Gas Prices in the UK

Gas Prices in the UK
Markets and Insecurity of Supply

PHILIP WRIGHT

Published by the Oxford University Press
For the Oxford Institute for Energy Studies
2006

OXFORD

UNIVERSITY PRESS

Great Clarendon Street, Oxford 0X2 6DP

Oxford University Press is a department of the University of Oxford.
It furthers the University's objective of excellence in research, scholarship
and education by publishing worldwide in

Oxford New York

Auckland Cape Town Dar es Salaam Delhi Hong Kong Karachi
Kuala Lumpur Madrid Melbourne Mexico City Nairobi
New Delhi Shanghai Taipei Toronto

with offices in

Argentina Austria Brazil Chile Czech Republic France Greece
Guatemala Hungary Italy Japan Poland Portugal Singapore
South Korea Switzerland Thailand Turkey Ukraine Vietnam

Oxford is a registered trade mark of Oxford University Press
in the UK and in certain other countries

Published in the United States
by Oxford University Press Inc., New York

British Library Cataloguing in Publication Data
Data available

Library of Congress Cataloguing in Publication Data
Data available

Cover designed by Clare Hofmann
Typeset by Philip Armstrong, Sheffield
Printed by The Alden Group, Oxford

ISBN 0-19-929965-X   978-0-19-929965-2

1 3 5 7 9 10 8 6 4 2

TABLE OF CONTENTS

LIST OF TABLES

LIST OF FIGURES

INTRODUCTION

This book is set in the context of considerable concern, expressed by both consumers and the UK parliament, about the recent volatility and high levels of UK wholesale gas prices. This concern has already led to an OFGEM[1] enquiry which had no sooner produced an interim report about the wholesale price spikes in the autumn of 2003, than it had to contend with an even more alarming spike in August 2004 which led to an upward surge in forward prices for the following winter. The latter immediately had a serious impact on domestic consumers as well as on the industrial and commercial consumers who are more exposed to wholesale markets. Partly informed by the findings of both OFGEM's interim report (published in May 2004) and its conclusions (published in October), the book has an underlying hypothesis which is implicit in its title, namely that it is insecurities of supply, mediated by markets, which have played an important role in the formation and behaviour of UK gas prices. However, while OFGEM has hunted the needle in the haystack to blame for unruly markets, our objective is to try to build a more comprehensive view of the causes of UK gas market behaviour.

We proceed under the premise that no basic concept which might be considered useful to this task – 'demand' or 'supply' or 'the market' – can be taken for granted in any generic form. Each has to be picked apart to expose its specificities as far as gas is concerned. The book is therefore organised, in its first three chapters, to establish what these specificities are before approaching the price data. The first chapter examines the main characteristics of UK gas demand and supply, including a conceptualisation of how they have been affected by liberalisation. Chapter 2 and Chapter 3 then focus on the organisation of the industry in terms of its ownership, marketplaces and contractual relationships. This will enable us to appreciate how the specific characteristics of the UK gas industry may, singly or in tandem, exercise their influence over price formation in different markets. We will thereby be exploring more 'systemic' or 'holistic' lines of causality. Such an approach, we believe, also insures against erroneous imputations of causality which might be the outcome of a purely number-crunching approach to the price data.

---

1 OFGEM (The Office of Gas and Electricity Markets) is the UK's regulatory body for the downstream gas and electricity industries.

Moving on to analyse the price data, Chapters 4 and 6 cover, respectively, wholesale and final prices, while Chapter 5, which addresses regulated transmission and distribution costs, provides the bridge between the two.

The overall result may still have some rough edges, but these partly reflect the fact that liberalisation is a fast moving target and that the data sources do not allow consistent chronological synchronisation. My hope, however, is that I have managed to map the territory in a way which others will find helpful for their work in or about the UK gas industry.

Philip Wright
University of Sheffield
October 2005

ACKNOWLEDGEMENTS

So many people and their organisations have helped me with this book. Jonathan Stern, Director of the OIES Gas Research Programme got me kick-started and read and commented on the complete draft. The Gas Research Programme's sponsoring company delegates also read draft chapters and provided feed-back at three valuable seminars as the book progressed. Two individuals in particular were always willing to share their considerable working knowledge of the UK gas market: Patrick Heren and Patrick Heather. Moreover, their respective organisations, Heren Energy and the International Petroleum Exchange, provided me with all the gas price data I could wish for but could not afford – their generosity in support of academic research, including the assistance of Martin Rose at Heren Energy and Jason Pegley and Stuart Wood at the IPE, has been exemplary. And they were not alone. Rhodri Thomas and Wood Mackenzie provided upstream data for which they are the only source, while Peter Osbaldstone, Louis Haycock, Rosie Cox, Simon Griew and Steve Thompson at National Grid Transco both provided data and gave their time to answer my numerous queries. Martin Thomas and Dawn Walters also freely provided and discussed APX data with me. Mike Earp, Clive Evans and Sara Atkins at the UK Department of Trade & Industry assisted with various official gas data series. Spending a day in the life of Tony Parkins, Robert Cross and Ian Lawrie at Statoil particularly helped incubate a fuller understanding of entry capacity auctions. Annie Reading at Centrica answered a crucial question. Howard Rogers at BP helped me crack one or two conundrums. Vicky Kiosse happily crunched a few numbers and the book could never be considered complete until Ian Rutledge, my long-term collaborator on numerous other projects, had passed judgment. To all of you my thanks, which also go to Judy Mabro for her expert edit and to Philip Armstrong for his work on the many figures.

CHAPTER 1

DEMAND, SUPPLY AND LIBERALISATION

Introduction

The role of this chapter is to introduce the characteristics of both the demand for and the supply of gas in the United Kingdom. This will enable us to identify the specific physical aspects of either demand or supply which may be of particular importance to price formation. Upon this picture we will then superimpose an analysis of the ways in which the liberalisation of the industry has affected the relationship between demand and supply.

The Demand for Gas in the UK

Scale

The first thing to note about demand for gas in the UK is that it has grown rapidly to make gas the dominant fuel within the country's overall energy demand. On an energy-supplied basis it contributed only 5.4 percent to UK primary energy consumption in 1970. By 1980, following its initial penetration of households and commercial and industrial applications it had grown to contribute 21.9 percent. The rise to 24 percent by 1990 reflected a relatively quiescent 1980s before it was let off the leash in power generation which, under the impetus of electricity privatisation and its accompanying 'dash for gas', drove gas' contribution up to 41 percent by 2000. In 2004 it was 42 percent (DTI 2005b). Gas is therefore the UK's most important energy source (oil, its nearest competitor, supplied only 32 percent of primary energy demand in 2004) but demand also appears to have reached a plateau, having been relatively stable at around 40 percent over the six years from 1998 to 2004.

Seasonal, Daily and Within-day Variations

If the overall importance of gas comes as no surprise, it will also be relatively obvious that the demand for gas in the UK, as in many other

1

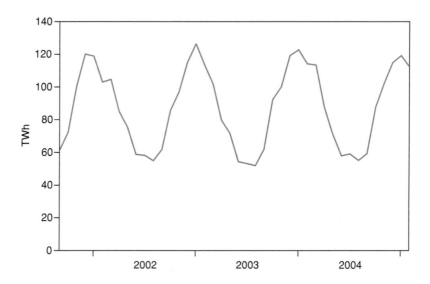

Figure 1.1: The Monthly Demand for Gas: September 2001 to February 2005

Source: DTI (2005b)

countries, is characterised by its *seasonality*. Changes in the seasonal demand for gas over the last three years are shown in Figure 1.1.

This reveals the very large seasonal swing in the demand for gas: an approximately 100 percent swing between peak demand in January and the level of summer demand. While other commodities are sold on markets that undergo even larger seasonal swings in demand – the demand for whisky, for example, regularly declines by about 200 percent between November and January (*Monthly Digest* 2004, Table 6.13) – gas is a much more important commodity. Gas has to be there on tap, wherever it is needed and in the quantities required at each moment of the day.

The demand for gas therefore also exhibits substantial *daily* and *within-day* variations. Daily variations give rise to the peak demands which the industry must be prepared to meet and these can be substantially greater than average monthly demand. For example, in January 2002, the peak monthly demand in Figure 1.1 breaks down into a daily average of 3,834 GWh/day. However, *peak* daily demand during the same winter period reached 5,693 GWh/day, almost 50 percent greater (National Grid Transco 2003). *Within-day variations*, although not as extreme as those confronting electricity, are nonetheless also important. While demand has a relatively flat profile during summer days and on cold winter days when space heating may be on continuously, during so-called 'shoulder' months like September and April demand can exhibit significant within-day variations as resort to space heating is only made at certain times of the day.

Composition

The long-term changes in the composition of the demand for gas are shown in Figure 1.2. They reveal both how important the growth in power station demand has been to the overall growth in demand since 1990, and how relatively stable has been the demand from other sectors. Indeed, with respect to the latter Transco notes (National Grid Transco 2003: 11−12) that gas use in these sectors has probably reached saturation point so that demand will only respond to either the weather or cyclical factors: by 2002 90 percent of homes in Britain were centrally-heated, with 80 percent of these installations being gas-fired, and gas's share of the domestic market had stabilised at around 68 percent between 1992 and 2002. Meanwhile, between 1997 and 2002 the penetration of gas in the industrial sector and in the service sectors had arrived at a plateau of around 45 percent of their energy demands.

A more detailed picture just for 2004 is given in Table 1.1. This shows that the largest component of the demand for gas is demand

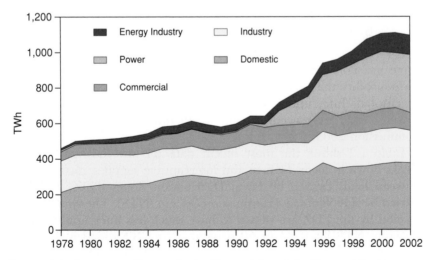

Figure 1.2: Long-term Changes in the Composition of the Demand for Gas

Source: National Grid Transco (2003)

from households, with demand for power generation a close second. The remaining, approximately one-third of demand is fragmented, with energy industry own use almost on a par with 'Other final users' who include commerce and public administration. Sixty-five percent of demand is 'intermediate' or 'derived' (all non-domestic uses) and 35 percent final (households).

Table 1.1: Composition of the Demand for Gas in 2004

	GWh	%
TRANSFORMATION	365,093	32.1
Electricity generation	345,694	30.4
Heat generation	19,398	1.7
Energy industry use	87,008	7.7
Losses	8,175	0.7
FINAL CONSUMPTION	677,036	59.5
Iron & steel	18,397	1.6
Other industries	145,492	12.8
Domestic	398,609	35.0
Other final users	103,877	9.1
Non energy use	10,660	0.9
TOTAL	1,137,312	100.0

Source: DTI (2005b)

Interruptible Demand

Some gas consumers pay less for their gas in return for accepting the possibility that, within certain agreed rules, their supplies may be interrupted. Interruption is at the discretion of the system operator (Transco) and may occur for up to 45 days per year (Competition Commission 2003: 84).[1]

Table 1.2 shows the most recent data on how UK gas demand breaks down in terms of firm and interruptible supplies, distinguishing between loads carried by Local Distribution Zones (LDZ) and loads carried by the National Transmission System (NTS). The smaller loads covered by the LDZ are shown to have much less interruptibility than the large NTS loads. Over 60 percent of the NTS load is for power stations, which also account for about a half of NTS interruptible

---

1   At the time of writing new contractual arrangements for interruption are being introduced as part of the new Unified Network Code.

supplies and a quarter of all interruptible supplies. Overall, about a fifth of UK consumption is shown to have been interruptible in 2004, a proportion which declined quite sharply in that year compared with 2002 and 2003.

Table 1.2: Firm and Interruptible Gas Supplies 2002–2004

	2002		2003		2004	
	TWh	*%*	*TWh*	*%*	*TWh*	*%*
LDZ LOAD	687		695		700	
Firm	577	84.0	591	86.0	598	87.0
Interruptible	110	16.0	104	15.1	102	14.8
NTS LOAD	420		442		398	
Firm	268	63.8	281	66.9	285	67.9
Interruptible	152	36.2	161	38.3	113	26.9
Power Generation Firm	160		168		187	
Power Generation Interruptible	68		56		57	
TOTAL CONSUMPTION	1,107		1,137		1,098	
Firm	845	76.3	872	78.8	883	79.8
Interruptible	262	23.7	265	23.9	215	19.4

Source: National Grid Transco (2005)

Short-term Substitutability

The extent to which gas demand may be rapidly substituted by other fuels is clearly critical to price formation, but for most consumers it is not an option. Consumers for whom it may appear to be an option are those whom we have just been discussing – consumers with interruptible contracts. However, the extent to which the existence of interruptible contracts is also an indicator of the extent to which gas can be rapidly substituted by other fuels depends on the answers to two questions. Firstly, how many interruptible customers have an alternative source of fuel? Secondly, for those that do have an alternative source, how long can they sustain its use? An answer of some sorts to the first question may be drawn from NERA's 2002 study which found that only 50 percent of interruptible customers surveyed had back-up fuel (NERA 2002) – which immediately implies that half of the gas consumers with interruptible loads can only interrupt by curtailing production or switching production to other plants.

For those who do have alternative fuel supplies, the second question comes into play – how long could they sustain an interruption? The nominal answer is 45 days – the standard level of allowable interruption in interruptible contracts. However, this is the maximum cumulative interruption over the course of a year: there is no expectation that a single interruption lasting 45 days would actually occur.

That this is the case may be illustrated by the most recent report from the Joint Energy Security of Supply working group (JESS) – which analyses the capability of the back-up supplies available to gas-fired electricity generators with interruptible contracts. According to this report 4.8 GW or 72 percent of CCGT capacity fuelled by transportation interruptible contracts has access to back-up fuel, while a further 0.9 GW has access to alternative gas sources via a direct pipeline connection to UK Continental Shelf (UKCS) gas fields. This leaves just 1 GW with no back-up capability (DTI 2004a: 36). However, for the large majority of power stations with interruptible contracts which do have back-up supplies (distillate), they would only have a brief life. Even if stocks of distillate were at their maximum, after 168 hours of continuous running half of the backed-up capacity would be lost. If stocks were at an average level, only a sixth of capacity would still have fuel to operate after the same period. The overall implication is that the alternative fuel supplies which support interruptible contracts are not able to offer *sustained* substitutability.

However, interruptibility as expressed via interruptible contracts is not the only form of interruptibility – some gas consumers are

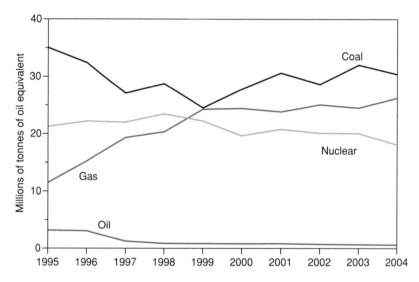

Figure 1.3: Fuels Used in Electricity Generation by Major Power Producers

Source for data: DTI (2005a)

demonstrably able and willing to 'self-interrupt' without any prompting from the system operator. These are principally power generators who self-interrupt in response to increases in the price of gas. This is achieved not by turning to the back-up supplies which may be available at gas-fired generating plant, but by substituting this plant with plant using other fuels.

Evidence that this has been happening is provided in Figure 1.3: coal was clearly being substituted for gas in both 2001 and 2003. That this could happen has been made possible by the portfolios of coal and gas generation plant held by five of the six major UK electricity generators.[2] Table 1.3 demonstrates not only this but also that their coal capacity is greater than their CCGT capacity. Given that their coal capacity is generally used 'mid-merit' (i.e. at less than full capacity) and their gas capacity is used as 'baseload', this means that they are capable of substituting all of their CCGT plant with their own coal capacity.

Quantifying the extent of the substitutability which this represents, if the five major generators were to simultaneously switch completely out of gas into coal, it would take 5.8 GW of CCGT capacity (i.e. excluding Didcot A) off the system. At a load factor of 71 percent (the average for the CCGTs operated by major electricity producers between 1999 and 2003) and using the 2004 transformation coefficient for gas to electricity, it can be calculated that this would reduce gas consumption by about 7 million tonnes of oil equivalent (mtoe) or almost 7 percent of total UK gas consumption in 2004. Even though overall system security, measured in terms of the surplus of available capacity over peak demand, need not be affected (the substituted plant could still be available to address an emergency), it is of course highly unlikely that such a large substitution would take place because of financial, operational, contractual and environmental constraints. Indeed, the substitutions out of gas which we have witnessed in 2001 and 2003 (Figure 1.3) have displaced only around half a mtoe gas. However, it does give some idea of the order of magnitude of the potential *sustainable* responsiveness to price which may be exercised directly and immediately.[3] Even at its theoretical maximum only a relatively small proportion of gas demand could be displaced by the most dynamic and price responsive UK consumers of gas, and in practice the actual proportion displaced has been less than 1 percent.

---

2   The generating company without a gas and coal portfolio is the nuclear generator, British Energy.

3   Other CCGT generators, without their own coal plant, can of course still arbitrage by making up their displaced production from the market. However, this strategy is more risky and will have transaction costs attached to it.

Table 1.3: UK Generators with Gas and Coal Capacity 2004

Company	Plant	Fuel	Capacity (Mw)
EdF Energy	Sutton Bridge	CCGT	803
	Cottam	coal	2,008
	West Burton	coal	1,972
E.ON (Powergen)	Kingsnorth	coal/oil	1,940
	Ironbridge	coal	970
	Ratcliffe	coal	2,000
	Connahs Quay	CCGT	1,380
	Cottam Development Centre	CCGT	400
International Power	Deeside	CCGT	500
	Rugeley	coal	1,006
RWE Innogy Plc	Aberthaw B	coal	1,455
	Tilbury B	coal/oil	1,020
	Didcot A	coal/gas	1,925
	Didcot B	CCGT	1,370
	Little Barford	CCGT	655
Scottish Power	Cockenzie	coal	1,152
	Longannet	coal	2,304
	Rye House	CCGT	715

Notes: **a)** the above data are as at end May 2004 (the DTI's census date) **b)** other generating capacity held by these companies using fuels other than gas or coal are excluded **c)** equity capacity which the companies may hold in gas-fired IPPs is excluded. The latter include EdF's indirect interest in Barking Power (installed capacity 1,000MW), Powergen's 50% interest in Corby Power (753MW) and 26.7% interest in Teesside Power (1,875MW), Scottish Power's 100% interest in Damhead Creek (792MW) and joint ownership of South Coast Power (400MW).

Source: DTI (2005a)

The Supply of Gas in the UK

The supply of gas in the UK, unlike for most countries in the European Union, is principally comprised of the country's own production from the UKCS. However, in 2004 the UK was on the cusp of again becoming a net importer, with consumption exceeding production for the first time since 1994. Seasonal and diurnal variations in demand are met from different forms of storage and also by imports. This means that the composition of the supply of gas varies according to the seasons and time of day and will be made up of beach supply plus or minus storage plus imports or minus exports. It is conventional to explore the contributions of these different sources of supply in terms of a 'Load Duration Curve', comprising a hierarchy of supplies which increasingly come into play up to the point at which everything is thrown into the pot in order to meet the demand which might occur on the coldest day in a 1 in 50 winter (see, for example, Competition Commission 2003: Figure 4.3, p.80). Here though we look at supply in terms of the dynamic combination of different sources over time – in order to lay the foundations for the analysis in subsequent chapters.

Figure 1.4 shows how production, storage, imports and exports have recently been interacting to meet the demand for gas in the UK. As is very evident, so-called 'beach swing' in UKCS production is of overriding importance to the country being able to meet winter demand. For example, during the winter of 2002/2003, the swing in beach supplies (from their lowest point in the summer of 2001) was about four times the largest monthly storage withdrawal deployed to meet peak winter demand. Other than the importance of beach swing, the other components of supply reveal a transition to net imports in the winter:

2001/02 and 2002/03	**2003/04 and 2004/05**
Summer months:	*Summer months:*
Stock building and net exports	Stock building and net exports
Winter months:	*Winter months:*
Stock run-down and little or no net imports	Stock run-down and net imports

So far, therefore, the impact of declining UKCS production is a seasonal one – declining peak supplies over the last three winters – such that the UK can no longer meet winter demand without the help of imports.

However, in the detail, we can already trace some of the developments which OFGEM has suggested contributed to the sharp rise in prices in October and November 2003: in October and November exports via the Interconnector continued despite the rise in UK prices (see also Figure 1.8), and there was consequently a sharp curtailment in stock-building in October. We shall return to this in Chapter 4 – here we move on to consider the different components of UK gas supply in greater detail, starting with the most important component, beach supply.

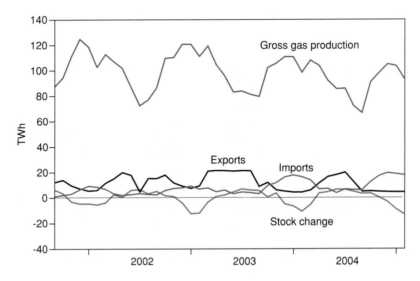

Figure 1.4: Monthly Variations in the Composition of UK Gas Supply,
September 2001 to February 2005

Source: DTI (2005b)

Beach Supplies and Beach Swing

Accompanying the peaking of UKCS gas production has been an
equally important development – the growth in the importance of 'Associated gas' (gas produced in association with oil) compared with 'Dry
gas' (gas produced from gas only fields), rising from under 50 percent
of landed production in 2001 to around 55 percent in 2002, 2003 and
2004 (Figure 1.5). Reflecting this, in 2003 eight of the ten fields which
produced 40 percent of the UK's gas (the rest is produced by about 240
other fields) were by then oil or gas condensate fields (DTI 2005d), the
other two being the Morecambe South and Morecambe North Dry gas
fields (which still accounted for 8.5 percent of gross output). Moreover,
the rise of Associated gas to become the predominant component of
beach supplies has also meant a geographical shift in the locus of
production from the southern basin of the North Sea to the oilfields
of the central and northern North Sea – and a corresponding rise in
the importance of the Teesside and St Fergus terminals, particularly
the latter, where gas from these areas is landed.

  The significance of this change is simply that the ability to control
and swing gas production from an oilfield is very much less than for a
Dry gas field. This in turn means that increasing reliance on Associated

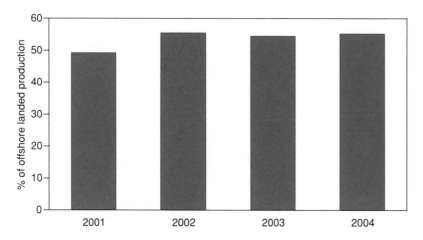

Figure 1.5: UKCS Landed Associated Gas Production as Percentage of Total Landed UKCS Gas Production

Source: calculated from DTI (2005e)

gas brings about both a reduction in *flexibility* and a potential reduction in the *reliability* of supplies. This is demonstrated or indicated in Figure 1.6. It is not only the case that the UK's Associated gas production shows very little swing capability compared with Dry gas production, but also that the pattern of Associated gas production reveals apparently random fluctuations around its trend (red line in Figure 1.6). While this is not of itself a conclusive indicator of reliability, it seems unlikely that these fluctuations are tightly orchestrated with both demand and other sources of supply. Whether because of technical problems or because of the requirements of sustaining flows of oil, the UK's supply of Associated gas therefore seems capable of administrating supply-side shocks to the UK gas market, as Figure 1.6 shows it certainly did in August and September 2004 (and which, like the October/November 2003 events, will be discussed in detail in Chapter 4).

Depleting Fields and Ageing Infrastructure

As well as the above shift in UK gas production towards a majority of Associated gas, thereby also pushing the centre of gravity of supplies northwards, individual field depletion and the age of UKCS offshore infrastructure are now seen as exercising a significant influence over price formation from the supply side. The detail of this argument will be explored in Chapter 4. Here suffice it to note that the depletion effect comes via unanticipated reductions in production and the ageing

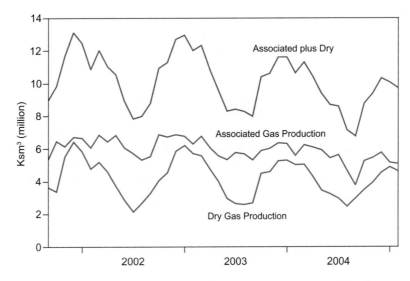

Figure 1.6: Monthly Variation in Total UKCS Production, Associated Gas
Production and Dry Gas Production: September 2001 to February
2005

Source: DTI (2005d)

infrastructure effect comes via increases in outages caused by both
planned and unplanned maintenance. The problem is that these effects
are difficult to distinguish from one another, and from the generally
less controllable flows of Associated gas production. Moreover, as
OFGEM has recently discovered, neither the government (the Department of Trade & Industry) nor the offshore industry (the UK Offshore
Operators' Association – UKOOA) has collated a historical record of
maintenance – which makes it difficult to establish whether maintenance
patterns in the recent past (which have now been collated) have been
on a rising trend (OFGEM 2004d: 38–40).

Imports and Exports

The first thing to note about the UK's foreign trade in gas is that until
the proposed new LNG import facilities come on stream its behaviour
is initially constrained by whatever is the current level of pipeline
capacity, and the direction of that capacity's flow. At present (mid-
2005) the UK is serviced by one major import pipeline, the Vesterled
pipeline from Norway which has a maximum capacity of about 13 bcm
(billion cubic metres) per year (National Grid Transco 2003) and lands
at St Fergus (thereby adding further to this terminal's importance). It

then has two dedicated export pipelines, the two Interconnectors to Ireland, which have a combined capacity of 11.5 bcm per year (344.53 MWh/day – DTI 2004a: 43). Finally, there is the bi-directional Bacton to Zeebrugge Interconnector which currently has an import capacity (reverse flow) of 8.5 bcm/year and an export capacity of about 20 bcm per year (Interconnector UK 2004).[4] The UK therefore has a foreign trade infrastructure which at one extreme is capable of importing a little under twice what it can export (with the Bacton Interconnector in reverse flow) and, at the other extreme (with the Bacton Interconnector in export mode), of exporting about two-and-a-half times what it can import. Maximum export capacity is roughly one-third and maximum import capacity is about one-fifth of UK domestic demand.[5]

While the overall result of the UK's foreign trade in gas is a seasonal swing between net exports during the summer months and an increasing need for net imports during the coldest winter months (Figure 1.7), the way in which this is achieved within the constraints of the UK's infrastructure adds considerable complexity to the profile of UK gas supplies (Figure 1.8).

In Figure 1.8 the red lines denote imports, either via the Interconnector (via Belgium, dotted line) or from Norway. Exports are in black, either via the Interconnector (dotted line) or to Ireland. The recent pattern has been one of steep increases in Norwegian imports to cover demand during the winter period, when imports via the Bacton Interconnector have been coming increasingly into play – net exports via the Interconnector are still positive but they dropped by 70 percent between 2003 and 2004. At the same time, the increasing demand for imports via the Interconnector increases the potential for conflict over the timing of imports and exports – while exports are seasonal, Figure 1.8 shows that the pattern which they have been following is not a stable one.

Storage and Lead Times

This brings us to the last component of UK supply, storage, which while it does not provide any net addition to supply over that afforded by UKCS production and net imports, does allow supply to be asynchronous with demand. Given the large variations in the demand

---

4   Alongside other major gas import infrastructure projects, the import (reverse flow) capacity of the Bacton Zeebrugge Interconnector is undergoing a two-stage upgrade to 16.5 bcm by December 2005 and 23.5 bcm by December 2006 (Interconnector 2004).

5   The data omit the export gas which flows directly from the UKCS to the Netherlands without being landed in the UK.

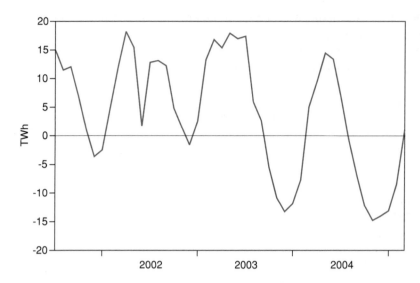

Figure 1.7: Monthly UK Net Exports (+) and Imports (–) of Gas

Source: DTI (2005e)

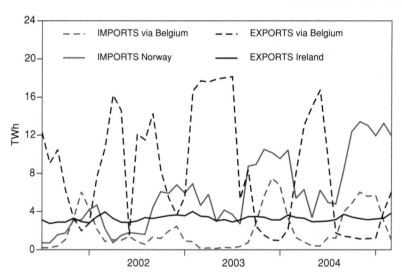

Figure 1.8: Recent Monthly Trends in UK Exports and Imports of Gas by
              Country

Note: The small amount of direct exports from the UKCS to the Netherlands are
omitted

Source: DTI (2005e)

for gas, it therefore becomes an important marginal component of supply at times of peak daily and seasonal demand. Table 1.4 details the capacity and operating characteristics of UK storage facilities as reported to the Competition Commission in 2003.

Table 1.4: The UK's Storage Facilities and their Characteristics

Facility	Space		Withdrawal			Refill Time from Empty
	Gwh	*%*	*GWh/day*	*%*	*Duration in days*	*Duration in days*
Depleted Field						
Rough	30,344	76.2	455	21.6	67	190
Hatfield Moor	1,260	3.2	55	2.6	23	
Salt Cavity						
Hornsea	3,495	8.8	195	9.3	18	
Hole House	300	0.8	30	1.4	10	
Five LNG Sites	3,846	9.7	769	36.5	5	192
Diurnal Storage	600	1.5	600	28.5	1	
TOTAL	39,845	100	2,104	100		

Source: Competition Commission (2003)

As well as providing the source for these data, the Competition Commission also offers probably the most succinct description of these facilities and their characteristics:

> Rough is substantially larger than the other sites in terms of space. Consequently its duration is also greater than that of the other high-deliverability storage sites. In particular the duration of Rough is far greater than that of the LNG facilities. Whilst the combined deliverability of the five LNG sites is very substantial (769 GWh a day), this level could only be sustained for five days and the sites would take 192 days to refill. By contrast, Rough could be nominated by customers at its nominal full deliverance, for 67 days and could then be refilled in approximately 190 days. This difference, together with the fact that the LNG injection process is considerably more costly per unit of gas stored and less flexible than that of Rough, makes Rough much more suitable than the LNG sites for seasonal storage and gives rise to very different usage patterns. The space provided by each of Hornsea, Hatfield Moor and Hole House is significantly less than that of Rough; the characteristics of these mid-range facilities fall broadly between those of Rough and the LNG sites. (Competition Commission 2003: para 4.105, p.85)

All that needs to be added to this passage, which sums up as 'more space less speed of delivery, more speed of delivery less space and longer refill', is that diurnal storage consists mainly of low pressure gas holders and transmission and distribution pipeline 'linepack' (storage made available by raising pipeline pressure above the minimum safe requirement; used by Transco to ensure the integrity of the system).

The ability of storage to respond to demand compared with other sources of flexible gas supply is estimated in Table 1.5. This information plus that which we have acquired from previous sections indicates that, apart from the Interconnector and LNG imports, all the UK's sources of flexible gas supply are technically capable of responding both rapidly and assuming a variety of loads to address particular levels of demand. However, whether they will do so is another question. For example, the Competition Commission's notes to the information in Table 1.5 read as follows with respect to the capabilities of Rough, Hornsea, the LNG sites, beach swing and the Interconnector:

> Lead time dependent on operational status. For Rough and Hornsea, the longer lead times may be needed if a change in direction of flow is required. For LNG, lead times depend on system configuration and linepack position. LNG injection may need to be pre-booked. For beach gas renomination lead times normally exceed 6 hours but vary depending on flow rates and contract terms. For the Bacton Interconnector, although shippers are only required to give 2 hours' notice, Transco's operational requirements can result in 5 to 8 hour lead times. Renominations needing a change in direction require a lead time of 48 hours. (Competition Commission 2003: 87)

Table 1.5: Estimated Response Times of the UK's Sources of Flexible Supply

Facility	Injection Lead Time	Withdrawal Lead Time
	Hours unless otherwise stated	
Depleted Field		
Rough	$2 \rightarrow 12$	$2 \rightarrow 12$
Hatfield Moor	1	1
Salt Cavity		
Hornsea	$2 \rightarrow 6$	$1 \rightarrow 6$
Hole House	Over 1	Over 1
Five LNG Sites	12 hours $\rightarrow$ 10 days	$1 \rightarrow 8$
Diurnal Storage	Immediate	Immediate
Other Sources of Flexibility	*Supply/Interruption Lead Time*	
Beach Swing	$6 \rightarrow 4$	
Bacton Interconnector	$2 \rightarrow 48$	
Interruptible Contracts	$3 \rightarrow 5$	
LNG Imports	$1 \rightarrow 10$ days	

Source: Competition Commission (2003)

This information not only indicates further technical complexity as the use of one form of storage (LNG) is shown to be constrained by aggregate system requirements and reversing flows introduces a stickier response, but also that other features of the system come into play: 'pre-booking', 'renominations', 'contract terms' and the fact that there is more than one shipper. These features in turn reflect the way the system is organised as an economic entity and take us into the impact of liberalisation on the relationship between demand and supply.

The Impact of Liberalisation

General Impacts on Demand and Supply

The preceding depiction of the demand for and the supply of gas in the UK highlighted three main characteristics relevant to price formation. Firstly, compared with most other European countries, it is relatively complex – principally because seasonality is mainly addressed by beach swing rather than from storage, but also because of the relationships between import and export flows and the physical infrastructure. Secondly, that swing itself is being affected by depletion, by the increasing predominance of Associated gas and by the ageing of UKCS infrastructure. Thirdly, on the demand side, there is only a limited degree of substitutability. Now we have to introduce a consideration of how liberalisation may affect the relationships between demand and supply as it atomises ownership, introduces different choices and marketises relationships which were previously administrative. Liberalisation is of course a process rather than a fixed policy package, a process which dates back to British Gas' first engagement with the Monopolies & Mergers Commission in 1988. Here however we restrict ourselves to its manifestation at the time of writing, leaving historical detail to make appearances in subsequent chapters.

To do so, it is helpful first of all to consider a benchmark contrast with the publicly-owned, vertically-integrated monopoly model of downstream supply and particularly to contend that, under this model, none of what we have so far learnt about the demand for and supply of gas would have had any direct and automatic implications for the price that consumers pay. For example, the occurrence of a short-term offshore supply shock under the publicly-owned, vertically-integrated model would not have made the news. British Gas would simply have made a technical decision to replace those lost supplies from the safest, most appropriate alternatives available, whether that be a storage option or swing from its in-house gas production. Any costs involved would simply have been absorbed as either normal to the operation or, if abnormal and persistent, they might eventually have found their way into consumers' bills. The important point however is that confronting such events was previously just a technical problem, albeit one with costs attached, and it was so because all of the choices were under the control of and at the disposal of one corporate entity.

Consider now the impact of liberalisation. Taking a very wide focus, liberalisation may be seen as having involved the introduction of a new legal framework, the de-integration of the industry ('unbundling' of what were seen as competitive activities, accompanied by owner-ship changes), the introduction of supply competition, the economic regulation of the residual monopoly 'core' (transportation) and the regulation, in conjunction with competition law, of the unbundled activities. In addition, the liberalisation of gas in conjunction with the liberalisation of electricity has transformed the relationship between the two industries, particularly given that one of the effects of the lat-ter, as we saw above, has been a dramatic increase in the importance of gas-fired generation. Here though, the focus is narrower – on the impact of liberalisation on the relationship between demand and sup-ply. Other aspects of liberalisation will feature in particular contexts in subsequent chapters, where there will also be operational detail about the consequences discussed below.[6]

On the demand-side, the main impact of liberalisation has been to offer consumers the new possibility of changing supplier. But in order for this to happen there has to be more than one supplier which also means a fragmentation in the ownership of supply. And if this happens there has to be some kind of Third Party Access to the transmission and distribution network for the new suppliers to be able to transport gas to their particular customers.

Stopping there for a moment, while the structural impact is con-centrated on the supply side the main impact on the relationship between demand and supply is to introduce much more uncertainty. Whereas previously the main uncertainty was the weather and the risk of offshore failure, now choice and competition mean that each supplier is much less certain of the level of demand from the customer who, from one moment to the next, and with the encouragement of OFGEM, may switch supplier. The first major ramifications of this uncertainty are both the need for daily gas balancing and the fact that it is likely to prove problematic. Unless they have specifically opted for

6   A wide-focus discussion of the liberalisation of the UK gas industry may be found in Wright (2005).

interruptible supply, customers require certainty that the amount of gas which they require at any particular moment in time will actually be delivered – something which the suppliers themselves are unable to achieve. Instead a system operator, in this case Transco, has to be put in charge of balancing the system, including the capability to acquire and dispose of gas in order to do so. But knowing how much gas to acquire or dispose of, and particularly when to do so during the day, is inevitably going to prove problematic because the system operator relies on information (in this case advance nominations) from shippers about their intentions. That it has proved problematic in fact is borne out by the voluminous regulatory documentation addressing this problem (e.g. OFGEM 2001a, 2002a, 2003a) – ultimately in vain because the problem of shipper and supplier uncertainty has simply been passed on to the system operator. It cannot be eliminated.

One way of addressing supply-side uncertainty is of course by holding stocks, but here too liberalisation has created a new kind of uncertainty. Gas storage has been hived off from transmission and distribution and then, in an effort to promote competitive pricing, it was further fragmented among different owners. Three inter-related problems have proved to be the consequence. Firstly, and as we have already demonstrated, the different forms of gas storage in the UK are neither substitutes for each other nor with non-storage substitutes such as beach swing. Each was created to address a particular technical problem encountered in delivering gas safely and in the right amounts at the right time. Each therefore has a virtual monopoly for its particular purpose, with the implication that suppliers will need to hold a portfolio of different kinds of storage, bought from owners who are not restrained by competition and who have proved difficult to regulate.[7] A supplier can still opt for one form of storage over another – gas after all is still gas wherever and however it may be stored. But then they may well be caught out: relying just on LNG, for example, will guarantee rapid deliverability, but it will not last long and takes as long as the giant Rough reservoir to refill.

Secondly, in the newly atomised and more uncertain marketplace created by liberalisation there is theoretically a need for a larger amount of stored gas than would be required under the publicly-owned, vertically-integrated monopoly model. However, two countervailing tendencies are simultaneously released by liberalisation. One of these is that stocks cost money and cost minimisation is a requirement of

---

7   For example, using auctions for storage capacity as a substitute for competition proved unattractive to the various owners of the Rough storage field – from BGplc through Dynegy to the current owners Centrica.

survival in a competitive market. The other is that the potential lack of customer loyalty to the supplier of a homogeneous product may make suppliers reluctant to book more than a minimum of storage.

Thirdly, if suppliers should theoretically need more storage capacity in a liberalised market then the owners of storage capacity would have to build and operate it. But again there are countervailing tendencies at work. One of these is that no storage owner will want to finance a surplus of storage capacity which will serve the collective good. A second one is that precisely because ownership is now fragmented there is a new risk that one particular owner may find that a disproportionate share of excess capacity unluckily falls to him, an effect akin to bearing stranded costs. A third one relates to a 'game' – everyone wants a free storage lunch provided by somebody else and there is therefore likely to be a reluctance to invest in storage capacity. All of these countervailing tendencies are likely to result in underinvestment in storage when more is actually required. Moreover, this conclusion is not undermined by the fact that the aggregate of proposed new storage developments in the UK amounts to 17,000 GWh, equivalent to over half the capacity of the Rough field (Competition Commission 2003: para 4.128, p.90). More storage will undoubtedly be required in the future as reduced beach swing and relatively inflexible imported supplies exercise their effect – but such future plans in no way indicate a concerted intent to create a surplus of storage capacity in the UK, and booking storage outside the UK is not a cost that suppliers appear willing to contemplate.

Let us finally combine liberalisation with the foreign trade choices which were identified above. These are now transformed from technical options into economic choices implying profit or loss. Moreover, as far as UK suppliers are concerned, we can also say that these opportunities mainly arise via use of the Bacton Interconnector which is not purpose-built for particular supplies and offers both export and import possibilities. However, the fact that its flow needs to be reversed in order to switch from export to import, that it can only do one or the other at a particular moment in time, makes for sticky responses to opportunities.

Markets and Contracts

Markets now mediate the transformed relationship between demand and supply but it would be a mistake to suggest that liberalisation is equivalent to either introducing the market to gas or that it creates anything as monolithic as 'the UK gas market'. Rather, liberalisation has both transformed existing market relationships and introduced new markets and market relationships which are constantly in flux. Moreover, these markets, either transformed or new, generate specific iterations between demand and supply and therefore specific price signals which are of interest to different participants for often quite different reasons. These price signals also differ in terms of temporality and in terms of the volumes over which they preside.

Working backwards from final consumers, there is first of all the retail market populated by domestic and small commercial and industrial customers. This has been transformed by supply competition. Then there is the larger-scale industrial and commercial market, again transformed by supply competition, dominated by contracts with suppliers (and often therefore referred to as the 'contract market'), but whose customers can also access wholesale markets directly or contract directly with the upstream. Then there are the various new short-term markets which may be transparent or embraced by 'Over-the-Counter' (OTC) trade.[8] They include a specific Within-day market created by OFGEM to allow shippers to trade out imbalances and Transco to acquire or signal the need for balancing supplies. This is the transparent 'On-the-Day Commodity Market' (OCM) which includes a market for the location-specific supplies needed to relieve locational, supply-side constraints. And then there is the futures market, its existence a recognition of the uncertainty created by liberalisation – which gives rise to the need for a market for hedging price risk. Finally, arriving at the upstream, there is a contract market between shippers/suppliers and producers and between the latter and final consumers – with risk management partially (at least with respect to volumes) subsumed within the contract.

The main point for the moment, however, is that these markets, and particularly the short-term markets, are capable of rapidly transmitting physical changes on the supply side, plus 'market sentiment' about them, into price signals, and of propagating them between themselves. This may in turn be considered the single most important distinguishing feature of a liberalised gas market – the sensitivity of price to changes in supply increases dramatically. Without wishing to jump ahead of ourselves, a brief example may immediately illustrate the complete contrast with the sequence of events which would have happened under the vertically-integrated, public monopoly model. Transco is busy trying to balance the system Within-day and has based its planning on Day-ahead flow nominations from shippers plus forecasts of demand based

---

8   OTC is the term used to describe trades which are customised confidentially between the parties concerned – in contrast to open-market trades which are standardised and priced transparently.

on weather and historical information. Then there is an unplanned interruption to offshore supplies affecting a particular shipper – who therefore under-delivers with respect to his Day-ahead nomination. Transco suddenly becomes aware of this development through monitoring On-the-day delivery flows and linepack levels and is compelled to make an unplanned balancing trade on the OCM, causing a sudden price rise. From the transparent OCM, this price rise then bounces into the OTC markets. The shipper who has made the paper balancing sale to Transco then draws down on his storage to make good his physical position, a move that is factored into the futures market because it happens in September, raising concerns that reduced stock levels may increase future resort to the spot markets at winter prices.

Ownership

By this point it may have become clear that as well as introducing the impact of liberalisation on the relationship between demand and supply, we have also been concerned to demonstrate the rationale for the content of subsequent chapters. One of these is about ownership. Ownership is important because it has the potential to create power on either the demand or the supply side – which in turn can have important implications for price formation. This has clearly been apparent with respect to the introduction of supply competition in the industrial market which, because it undermined the power of the incumbent seller, also increased buyer-side power – turning the industrial market into a rather unhappy, unprofitable place for suppliers to do business. It has also been apparent in the urge to create a powerful corporate position on the demand and the supply side, and if possible in electricity as well, as a perfectly rational response to a market in which consumers above all require security while supply and demand are characterised by complex and interacting uncertainties.

Regulated Costs

Finally, a word about regulated costs, which are addressed in Chapter 4. An important, but often overlooked feature of liberalised gas markets, is that a large chunk of costs, those comprising the cost of using the transmission and distribution network, have not been liberalised, but are still subject to economic regulation. This is important for three main reasons. First of all, it can create an illusion as far as price formation is concerned: consumers may see price reductions which they ascribe to the efficiency of markets and competition when the reality is that such reductions may have occurred because of regulatory intervention. This is the case because transmission and distribution can account for a large proportion of final prices (around 30 percent for residential consumers). Secondly, and relatedly, depending on the scale of transmission and distribution costs they also provide partial insulation against movements in the wholesale price of gas. Thirdly, because transmission and distribution costs are very different for different categories of consumer, particularly for residential consumers compared with industrial and commercial consumers, the effect of the illusion and the insulation are different in different markets.

CHAPTER 2

THE OWNERSHIP OF THE UK GAS CHAIN

Introduction

In this chapter we seek to establish the ownership of the UK gas chain from the well-head to the interface with the final consumer. This will take in producers, major pipeline owners, terminal owners, storage owners, shippers and suppliers. As well as seeking to establish ownership of these individual functions in the chain, at the end of the chapter we shall bring them together in company portfolios in order to view ownership from the perspective of the entire gas chain. We shall also consider the horizontal ownership relationships which have been established with the UK's Electricity Supply Industry. The purpose is twofold. First of all, and given that market relationships express power relationships rather than a neutral coming together of anonymous 'market forces', we wish to discover whether particular companies or groups of companies have established positions of power in the UK gas chain, and what the nature of that power is. However, this is not done under an *a priori* assumption that such power will be or can necessarily be used to the detriment of the consumer. Moreover, power may be unrelated to company size − as we shall see later, the UK gas market may easily be disturbed by relatively small events if these happen in the wrong place at the wrong time. Secondly, we wish to expose how companies have organised their portfolios in the gas chain, and the implications which this may have for managing price risk/containing profit risk and therefore their ability or willingness to create and respond to price signals.

The Upstream

The creation of the UK's offshore oil and gas industry has been an astonishing feat of engineering which the country's citizens are only dimly aware of and only concerned about as the beginning of its demise brings home the risks to which the country may be exposed without it. As of August 2004, it comprised 84 oil platforms, 18 floating installations and 166 gas platforms (DTI 2005d). Given that nearly

24

all the oil platforms produce Associated gas, there was a total of 247 fields producing gas from the UKCS. Moreover, this feat has been the work of a relatively small number of companies, particularly the oil majors, and their employees, some of whom have paid with their lives in dangerous and difficult working conditions.

Although the ownership of individual fields has provided the data which we shall present, it is not necessary for our purpose to laboriously rehearse this on a field-by-field basis. Rather we are interested in two questions. Firstly, what is the company structure of production – how much does each company produce and how important is it? Secondly, what is the company structure of *control over production* (quite different from the first question, as we shall see)?

Production

Determining UKCS gas production on a company-by-company basis is not at all straightforward. First of all, there is the question of 'what is production'? Gross production usually refers to well-head production, from which own-use for production and power will be deducted to arrive at a figure for 'landed' or 'marketed' production – sometimes also referred to as 'net production' (by the UK's Department of Trade & Industry, for example).[1] Then, whichever definition of production is adopted, company production has to be calculated by summing the equity share of production which a company holds in each field in its portfolio. While the UK's Department of Trade & Industry does provide up-to-date data on the ownership of individual gas-producing fields, and on gross gas production by field, it only provides partial data on landed or marketed production on a field-by-field basis. We therefore rely on data from Wood Mackenzie which are drawn directly from producing companies. Comparing Wood Mackenzie's total gas production for 2003, arrived at by summing its company data, with the DTI's total for net (landed) production, they are close enough (within 3 percent) to believe that the Wood Mackenzie data provide a reasonable estimate of company landed or marketed gas (see Table 2.1).

This table reveals that UK gas production is highly concentrated, with just seven companies, five of which are oil majors, accounting for about three-quarters of production. However, no company has an overwhelmingly dominant position with production being fairly equally distributed among the top producers. Beyond the cut-off point of 1bcm

---

1   Other authorities in the world, such as Cedigaz, include flared gas in gross production. However, this is not the practice of the UK's Department of Trade & Industry.

Table 2.1: Company Gas Production from the UKCS in 2003

Company	% of UKCS Production	Cumulated %	BCM per annum
ExxonMobil	13.3	13.3	14.0
BP	12.9	26.2	13.5
Centrica	10.4	36.6	10.9
TotalFinaElf	10.4	46.9	10.8
Shell	10.2	57.2	10.7
ConocoPhillips	8.8	66.0	9.2
BG	8.0	74.0	8.3
ChevronTexaco	3.4	77.4	3.6
ENI	3.3	80.7	3.5
Perenco	2.8	83.6	3.0
Amerada Hess	2.8	86.4	2.9
Marathon	2.1	88.5	2.2
BHP Billiton	2.0	90.5	2.1
Gaz de France	1.5	92.0	1.5
Consort Resources	1.2	93.1	1.2
Talisman	1.1	94.2	1.2
Kerr-McGee	1.1	95.3	1.1
Tullow Oil	0.9	96.3	1.0

Source: Wood MacKenzie (2004)

of production which embraces the above list of 18 companies, there are 26 other companies producing very small amounts of gas.[2]

Control over Production

The question of control over production has three dimensions: operatorship of offshore fields, Dry versus Associated gas production, and contracts. Company operatorship of fields is important because it is the company that operates an offshore field which is in day-to-day control of production decisions and has responsibility for confronting the consequences of breakdowns and accidents. Whether this operatorship is over Dry or Associated gas production is important firstly because, as we saw in Chapter 1, it is the Dry gas fields which provide the lion's share of swing to meet peak winter demand. Secondly, Associated gas production is less amenable to control, being subordinate to

---

2   Since this section was originally drafted Woodmac has made available the 2004 data. However, it was decided not to update both because the 2004 company profile of UKCS gas production is broadly unchanged compared with 2003, and in order to retain a reasonably close alignment with the available ownership data for downstream supply.

maximising liquids production. Contracts are important because if they are 'buyer-nominated', control in effect passes from the producer to the wholesale customer. Here we shall only assess the first two aspects of control, leaving contracts to be discussed in the more appropriate context of Chapter 3.

Table 2.2 shows some important differences compared with the

Table 2.2: Dry and Associated Gas Production: Proportions of Total Controlled by Operator Companies

Operators	Dry	Associated
Amerada Hess	-	0.0
BG	5.3	6.0
BHP Billiton	5.8	0.1
BOL (Chevron/ConocoPhillips)	-	10.3
BP	7.1	21.0
Burlington Resources	2.2	-
CNR		1.3
Centrica	22.3	-
ConocoPhillips	16.0	5.9
Caledonia	0.8	-
Gaz de France	0.5	-
Encana	-	0.3
ENI	0.5	0.4
ExxonMobil	2.9	9.6
Kerr-McGee	-	0.3
Marathon	-	11.9
Perenco	8.5	-
Petro-Canada	-	0.5
RWE	0.3	-
Shell	19.4	15.4
Statoil		0.8
Talisman	-	1.0
ChevronTexaco	-	2.0
TotalFinaElf	4.6	13.1
Tullow	3.3	
Venture	0.7	0.2
	100.0	100.0

Source: the data in this Table were calculated by the author using the 2003 gross gas production of gasfields which land/market gas in the UK. This should therefore only be taken as an approximation because the use of gross gas production will clearly overstate landed/marketed production. However these are the only data available with which to match companies with production for this purpose. The fields were identified using DTI data (from DTI 2005d) supplemented by the more detailed information available from the Ninth Edition of OPL's North Sea Field Development Guide (2003).

ownership of UKCS gas production. First of all, the control of Dry gas production is highly concentrated with only two companies, Centrica and Shell, controlling over 40 percent. Adding just one more company, ConocoPhillips, the proportion rises to almost 58 percent. The control of Associated gas production is, like the ownership of gas production in general, more dominated by a handful of oil majors, with six of them controlling over 80 percent of the total. However, BP did emerge as the dominant company in this group – operating over a fifth of Associated gas production in 2003. Another point to note is that one company, BOL (the Chevron/ConocoPhillips partnership) controls over 10 percent of the UK's Associated gas production from one field, Britannia. Considering operatorship of both Dry and Associated gas production, in 2003 Shell had strong positions in both and therefore emerged as the company with potentially the most powerful influence over UKCS gas production.

Pipelines and Terminals

Pipelines and terminals are, unsurprisingly, owned and operated by major upstream producers. Table 2.3 shows the relatively diffuse, collaborative ownership of offshore pipelines, reflecting both the large-scale investment required to construct them and a concern to have primary access rights in their use. However, it should also be borne in mind that the advantages conferred by ownership of offshore pipeline infrastructure are now constrained by the extension to the offshore of the third party access rights enjoyed onshore. While there is some historical legislative underpinning to this right of access, it is essentially driven by a voluntary Code of Practice drawn up by the UK Offshore Operators' Association in conjunction with the Department of Trade & Industry and published in August 2004 (UKOOA 2004). Access is therefore negotiated under this Code rather than regulated in the manner of the onshore regime. Fifty UKCS companies have signed up to the Code covering twenty major pipeline systems and including 'all major pipelines operated by BP, ChevronTexaco, ConocoPhillips, ExxonMobil, Shell, Talisman and Total' (Dymond 2005).

Table 2.4 identifies the terminal operators and the proportion of peak demand they are responsible for. Shell emerges as the largest operator with just over a quarter of peak flow, followed by TotalFinaElf with 17.4 percent. The data also quantify the point made in Chapter 1 about the migration of gas landings northwards as associated gas from the central and northern North Sea has come to predominate

Table 2.3: Major UKCS Gas Pipelines and their Owners

Pipeline	*Owners*
VESTERLED	GASSLED Partners (Norwegian State via Petoro AS 38.293%; Statoil 20.379%; Norsk Hydro 11.134%; Total 9.038%; ExxonMobil 9.755%; Shell 4.681%; Norsea Gas 3.018%; ConocoPhillips 2.033%; ENI 0.862%; Fortum Petroleum 0.807%)
FLAGS (Far North Liquids and Associated Gas System)	Shell/ExxonMobil
SAGE (Scottish Area Gas Evacuation)	ExxonMobil (25%), Marathon (19%), BP (13.85%), Shell (11.39%), Amerada Hess (11.10), Talisman (9%), Kerr-McGee (4%), Nippon Oil Corporation (3.15%), OMV (2.5%), ENI(1%)
CATS (Central Area Transmission System)	BG (51.18%), BP (29.53%), Amerada Hess (17.72%), ConocoPhillips (0.66%), TotalFinaElf (0.57%), ENI (0.34%)
SEAL (Shearwater and Elgin Area Line)	ExxonMobil (22.434%), TOTAL (19.679%), Shell (12.6%), ENI (12.029%), BP (12.375%), BG (7.761%), GdF (5.715%), E.ON Ruhrgas (2.86%), ChevronTexaco (2.145%), Dyas (1.205%), Oranje Nassau Energie (1.205%)
BRITANNIA	BOL (ChevronTexaco/ConocoPhillips)
MILLER	BP(60%), ConocoPhillips(25%), Shell(15%)
FULMAR	Shell (50%), ExxonMobil (50%)
IRELAND INTERCONNECTOR	BGE
BACTON INTERCONNECTOR	Amerada Hess 5%;BP 10%; BG 25%; ConocoPhillips 10%; Distrigas 10%; ENI 5%; EON Ruhrgas 10%; International Power 5%; Gazprom 10%, TotalFinaElf 10%

Source: Company information; Wood Mackenzie (2004)

over Dry gas: at peak flow about half of UK gas is being landed through St Fergus and Teesside, with the former alone responsible for 38 percent.

Table 2.4: Operatorship of the UK's Pipeline Terminals

Sub-terminal & Operator	Maximum Winter Daily Flow 2003–04 (mcm)	% of Total
St Fergus Frigg – TotalFinaElf	68.6	17.4
St Fergus SAGE – ExxonMobil	52.6	13.3
Bacton – Shell	45.4	11.5
Barrow – Hydrocarbon Resources (Centrica)	44.8	11.4
Teesside CATS – BP	30.1	7.6
Theddlethorpe – ConocoPhillips	30.1	7.6
St Fergus FLAGS – Shell	29.8	7.6
Bacton SEAL – Shell	29.3	7.4
Dimlington – BP	17.6	4.5
Teesside CATS – TGPP (ex-Enron)	14.4	3.7
Bacton – Perenco	12.5	3.2
Bacton – Tullow	8.3	2.1
Easington Amethyst (sub-terminal, no processing)	6.6	1.7
Easington – BP	4.1	1.0
TOTAL	394.2	100.0

Note: Point of Ayr, operated by BHP Billiton, would usually be included in the list of UK terminals. The fact that OFGEM chose to exclude it for the purpose of this analysis is presumably because of the relatively small amount of gas which it is responsible for handling, such that it could not have played a significant role in contributing to supply-side shocks.

Source: OFGEM (2004a: Figure 4.4b, p.21); DTI (2005e)

Storage

The characteristics of UK gas storage have already been referred to in Chapter 1. Here we introduce the ownership of the facilities identified in Table 1.4.

Table 2.5 reveals Centrica's overwhelming dominance of storage space and Transco's dominance of withdrawal capability. Two further points need to be noted. Firstly, Centrica's dominance of storage space via its ownership of Rough is constrained by the undertakings required by the Competition Commission following its investigation of the implications of its acquisition of Rough from Dynegy in November 2002. These include requirements that it sell all of Rough's capacity on non-discriminatory terms and that it reserve no more than 20 percent of capacity for itself in the first year (2004/05), subsequently falling to a maximum of 15 percent over five years (Competition

Table 2.5: The Ownership of UK Storage Facilities

Facility	Owner	Space %	Withdrawal %	Duration in days
Depleted Field				
ROUGH	Centrica	76.2	21.6	67
HATFIELD MOOR	Scottish Power/ Edinburgh Oil & Gas	3.2	2.6	23
Salt Cavity				
HORNSEA	SSE	8.8	9.3	18
HOLE HOUSE	EdF	0.8	1.4	10
FIVE LNG SITES	Transco LNG	9.7	36.5	5
DIURNAL STORAGE	Transco	1.5	28.5	1
TOTAL	39,845	100	100	

Source: Competition Commission (2003)

Commission 2003: 5). Secondly, while ScottishPower/Edinburgh Oil & Gas, EdF and SSE may appear to be minor players, the speed with which these facilities may be accessed and refilled (Table 1.5) make them strategically important vehicles for responding to price signals.

Transmission, Distribution and Shipping

Transmission and Distribution

A brief ownership history of the UK's gas transportation system is that it became Transco within British Gas in 1994, was unbundled into BG plc in 1997 (Centrica, trading as British Gas, assumed the divested supply business), then divested from BG into the Lattice Group in 2000 before finally joining National Grid – which became National Grid Transco in 2002. In addition, Transco's status as the unitary opera-tor of the system has been challenged by two developments. Firstly, following an amendment to the 1986 Gas Act by the 1995 Act, there is now a small number of independently licensed pipeline companies known as Independent Gas Transporters (IGTs). IGTs are pipeline systems connected directly to Transco's system via a Connected System Entry Point (CSEP) or indirectly via another IGT. Both business and domestic customers are served by IGTs but the vast majority of their customers are domestic households on new housing estates where, by definition, there were no existing connections to Transco's system. By 2001, there were ten IGTs serving 238,254 customers (compared with around 20 million attached to Transco's system). However, OFGEM has estimated that IGTs are gaining around 60 percent of connections to new premises and by the end of 2005 the number of consumers connected to IGTs might reach 500,000. The companies involved and their customer numbers in 2001 are shown in Table 2.6.

In a number of cases, IGTs are part of a larger energy company. Scottish Power Gas Pipelines is owned by Scottish Power UK plc; British Gas Connections is owned by Centrica plc, Britain's largest gas supply company; East Midlands Pipelines is owned by PowerGen plc, itself owned by E.ON A.G.; Utility Grid Installations is owned by state-owned Bord Gas Eireann; and SSE Pipelines is owned by Scottish & Southern Energy plc. These parent companies are multi-utilities, most of which have interests in electricity supply, and/or gas supply, electricity generation and electricity distribution and in some cases have upstream gas assets.

Table 2.6: Independent Gas Transporters and their Customer (supply point) Numbers at April 1, 2001

IGT	Supply Points
Independent Pipelines Ltd	130,000
The Gas Transportation Company Ltd	49,250
British Gas Connections Ltd	34,120
Scottish Power Gas Ltd	15,523
SSE Pipelines Ltd	6483
E.S. Pipelines Ltd	1
East Midlands Pipelines Ltd	2,662
United Utilities Gas Pipelines Ltd and United Utilities Gas Networks Ltd	214
Utility Grid Installations Ltd	1
Mowlem Energy Ltd	0
TOTAL	238,254

Notes: Independent Gas Pipelines was formerly known as TotalFinaElf Pipelines Ltd and before that, AGAS Developments Ltd. The Gas Transportation Co. Ltd holds two separate GT licences. Both of the United Utilities companies are owned by the parent company United Utilities plc.

Source: OFGEM (2002c)

Secondly, and much more important, in August 2004 National Grid Transco announced the sale (subject to regulatory approval which has since been granted) of four of its regional gas distribution networks: the North of England network to a consortium led by Cheung Kong Infrastructure Holdings Ltd (and which includes United Utilities), Wales & the West to a consortium led by an Australian bank (Macquarie European Infrastructure Fund) and the South of England and Scottish networks to a consortium comprising Scottish and Southern Energy (SSE), Borealis Infrastructure Management Inc and the Ontario Teachers Pension Plan (National Grid Transco 2004). National Grid Transco retains the West Midlands, London and the East and North West of England, and therefore still remains by far the largest distribution business with 11 million home and business customers. However, the sales do raise important questions both about the development of new patterns of multi-utility ownership and about the vertical reintegration of the network itself at the hands of Scottish & Southern Energy (Table 2.7). Although it has already happened in the UK Electricity Supply Industry, this latter development would at one time have seemed inconceivable because the unbundling of the UK gas industry to separate out 'monopoly core' transportation from the potentially

Table 2.7: Distribution Networks and their Purchasers

Distribution Network	*Purchaser*	*Purchasers' other activities*
Scotland	Scottish & Southern Energy plc + Ontario Teachers Pension Plan + Borealis	Gas and electricity supply in Scotland, South of England and Wales.
		Electricity distribution in Scotland
		Electricity generation in Scotland
South of England	Scottish & Southern Energy plc + Ontario Teachers Pension Plan	As above
North of England	United Utilities plc +	Electricity and water distribution in North West England.
	Cheung Kong Holdings	Management of water distribution in Wales
Wales and South West	Macquarie Bank	Water distribution in South East England via South East Water plc

competitive supply business seemed to be the essential ingredient of liberalisation – rendering the ownership of transportation both unavailable to gas companies with other functions in the chain (regulatory approval seemed unlikely to be granted) and also uninteresting for them (under a third party access regime vertical integration seemed to offer no tangible benefits). It remains to be seen what the implications will be for UK gas consumers. Meanwhile it is interesting to note how the market seems to be taking both the gas and the electricity industries back towards vertical integration.[3]

Shipping

While OFGEM (2004c) lists a total of 71 licensed gas shippers in the UK, in Table 2.8 we use an April 2005 membership list from the OCM (On-the-Day Commodity Market). This is because all OCM members must have shippers' licences and OCM members are those licensees who are *actively* involved in trading and shipping. They are mainly energy companies involved in downstream supply, but the list does also include three other categories of shipper/trader: financial institutions (Barclays, Merrill Lynch, J.Aron[4]), upstream producers from the UKCS who do not have downstream supply companies (e.g. BHP) and trading companies (e.g. Cargill and Vitol, the latter a colourful Swiss company mentioned by the Iraq Survey Group in connection with oil smuggling and also embroiled in a contractual controversy in Kenya – Iraq Survey Group 2004; Kisero 2004).

Supply

At one level the ownership of supply is conceptually straightforward – it simply involves discovering which companies sell to final consumers (either to household or to industrial and commercial customers) and how much they sell, a task which OFGEM accomplished not too long

---

3   Indeed on its website EdF Energy positively glows about the advantages of an industry structure which is increasingly coming to resemble that of the original state-owned structure which so much time and effort has been spent in replacing – 'As one of the largest regulated and private networks operators in the UK we distribute electricity to over a quarter of the country's population. We are one of the few vertically integrated companies, which means we manage energy from the moment it's harnessed, to the second it's used, with expertise in generation, distribution and supply.'

4   J.Aron is the commodities division of Goldman Sachs.

Table 2.8: Members of the On-the-Day Commodity Market (OCM)
(as of April 2005)

Accord	AEP
Amoco	Arco British
ATEL	Barclays Bank
BG International	BHP Billiton
Bord Gais Eireann	BP Exploration
BP Gas Marketing	British Energy
British Gas Trading	Britoil
Cargill	Centrica Storage
ConocoPhillips	Coolkeeragh ESB
Corona	Deeside Power
E.ON	EdF Energy
EdF Trading	Electrabel
Electricity Supply Board	Enfield Energy
ENI	Essent
ExxonMobil	Foundation Energy
Gaselys	Gaz de France
Gazprom	Glencore Energy
Hess Energy	Hydro Energy
Intergen	J. Aron
Magnox Electric	Marathon Oil
Merrill Lynch	Natural Gas Shipping
Regent Gas	Ruhrgas
RWE	Scottish Power
Sempra	Shell
Smartestenergy	Spalding Energy
SSE Energy Supply	Statoil
Total	Transco LNG
Transco	Utilita
Vitol	Wingas

Source: APX Gas (2005a)

ago, the results of which we shall introduce below. However, there is another level, potentially very important to price formation, but which is complex, layered and elusive. Can ownership be discovered as upstream production is converted into supply for final consumers?

Routes to Market, Ownership and Power

The most distant layer from the downstream market is ownership as upstream producers sell their equity production. At this point, market shares would correspond to those identified in Table 2.1 – with seven companies, led by ExxonMobil, controlling three-quarters of the market. However, the subsequent layers become tangled, simply because gas supplies from the upstream then take different routes to market, depending upon to whom the upstream producers sell their gas. Figure 2.1, which was drawn up after discussions with two major, but quite different upstream producers, attempts to capture the possibilities. It reveals five potential routes to market from the upstream:

1.   Direct to final customers
2.   To a downstream supply company which is another upstream company
3.   To a downstream supply company which is a subsidiary
4.   To a downstream supply company which is not a producer
5.   To the wholesale market

Even without the further complexity added by different combinations of these routes, and by the interchanges between them, it is immediately apparent that attempting to capture an impression of market power by way of ownership shares between the upstream and the downstream is impossible. All that we can do is to provide some illustrative evidence of the extent to which the different routes are used and of the strategies adopted by different companies.

The first point to make is that route 1, direct sales from the upstream to final customers, is apparently small and diminishing – restricted to a small amount of gas tied up in expiring 'legacy' contracts. Secondly, and unavoidably pre-empting some of the content of Chapter 3, the sales to downstream supply companies comprise two elements: sales under

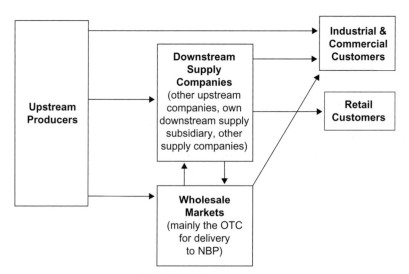

Figure 2.1: Engagement of the Upstream with the Downstream

'old fashioned', 'beach' contracts (estimated in Figure 3.8, Chapter 3 to cover about 44 percent of throughput in 2004) and long-term contracts for delivery to National Balancing Point (NBP). There is no source of data to offer precision about the latter – all that is known with certainty is that the volume of gas sold via wholesale markets (mainly the 'Over-the-Counter' market – OTC) + long-term contracts for delivery to NBP covered about 56 percent of throughput in 2004.

Illustrating the routes to market with actual company strategies brings other features of the engagement between upstream and downstream into play. Here a point which has been reiterated to the author many times must preface all others. This is that upstream producers generally have an 'engineering outlook' – the economics of operations extend over the lifetime of their fields and they are simply concerned to maximise production, not to vary their production or interventions in the market for short-term speculative gains. This in turn means that a number of producers, notably ConocoPhillips, BG plc, Chevron and Marathon are only concerned to dispose of their production, either by way of contracts with other producers for delivery to NBP, or on the OTC. Other companies, distinguished by the fact that they do have downstream supply operations, notably Total, BP and Shell, actively trade on wholesale markets. However, this does not necessarily imply that their upstream operations either deviate from the 'engineering out-look' or discriminate in favour of their downstream arm via preferential sales.[5] The upstream arm of at least one of these companies simply disposes of all its output over and above its legacy contracts on the OTC, leaving its downstream arm to make its own arrangements.[6]

These general points about strategy, which reveal that there are not only different routes to market, but also different ways of using them (particularly as either active or passive traders) may now be quantified for three companies in a way that exposes another dimension of the conversion of upstream production into downstream supply. The three companies are ExxonMobil, BP and Centrica which, in the context of the relationships described in Figure 2.1, are interesting because they represent three different kinds of 'deficit company'. ExxonMobil states that 'Sales in the UK are approximately 20 billion cubic metres of gas

---

5   Preferential sales involving discounts would in any event be unlikely: they would go against the logic of the internal dismemberment of companies into autonomous business units, they would be likely to attract the attention of the regulatory authorities and taxation of the upstream is in any event based on imputed revenues calculated using market prices.

6   For reasons of confidentiality the name of this company cannot be dis-closed.

per year' and 'Gas is sold to a range of customers including the power generation industry, and also gas distribution companies, who re-sell gas to customers in the industrial, commercial and domestic sectors' (ExxonMobil 2004). This means that ExxonMobil is selling more gas in the UK than it produces from the UKCS (14 bcm in 2003, see Table 2.1). Because it has no downstream supply operation it may therefore be categorised as a 'deficit producer', one which may source its deficit from Norwegian production, from other UKCS producers or from the OTC.

BP states that in 2003 it sold 26.9 billion cubic metres of gas into the UK market of which 15.5 bcm was from its own production (BP 2004). This means that BP is both selling much more than it is able to source from its own production and more than it produces from the UKCS alone (13.5 bcm in 2003 – Table 2.1). Unlike ExxonMobil, however, BP is also a supplier of gas to industrial and commercial customers. It may therefore be categorised as a 'deficit producer/supplier', although its October 2004 decision to reduce its downstream supply operations by withdrawing from the smaller-scale end of the industrial/commercial market (Thorniley 2004) may indicate that it is moving towards becoming a deficit producer like ExxonMobil.

Centrica sold, under the British Gas brand, approximately 24 bcm into the UK market in 2003 (calculations based on data in Centrica 2003), the vast majority of which (20.9 bcm) was to residential customers. Given that Centrica's own production in 2003 was 10.9 bcm (Table 2.1), this means that Centrica relied on other upstream producers for a majority (55 percent) of its supplies. However, Centrica is not primarily an upstream producer, it is a downstream supply company with upstream interests – such that it is better categorised as a 'deficit supplier/producer'.

These examples tell us that these three companies alone are net buyers to the extent of over 31 bcm (a little under a third of the UK market), but we also know that the manner in which this might translate into power (or lack of it) with respect to price formation depends on exactly how the deficits are sourced (own production from outside the UKCS, contracts with other upstream producers or via wholesale markets). Secondly, while these examples might also seem to indicate a major 'pre-concentration' of sales as upstream production is converted into downstream supply, we have previously noted that it is impossible to draw such a conclusion because there is in fact no common denominator for the companies' sales and, relatedly, double-counting could well be involved (e.g. if Centrica is buying wholesale gas from ExxonMobil or BP). Meaningful quantification of market shares is only possible with respect to final consumers, either non-domestic or domestic, and to these we now turn.

Non-domestic Market Shares

The most recent detailed market share data for this group of final consumers come from a competition review published by OFGEM in 2003 which compiled data for 2002. This was the first time that such data were published in detail and, because of its commercial sensitivity its publication was preceded by consultation with the companies concerned. The result, the details of which were published as an OFGEM decision (OFGEM 2003c), implied full disclosure but for the non-domestic market disclosure takes the two forms represented in Tables 2.9 and 2.10 and these do not allow the matching of a specific market share to a particular company. The decision also promised a quarterly update to be published on OFGEM's website, but this does not appear to have been done.

Nevertheless a number of interesting features about the non-domestic market emerge by combining the information in Tables 2.9 and 2.10. First of all, 72 percent of the Small market (<50,000 therms) is held by British Gas (Centrica), Powergen and TotalFinaElf, 56 percent of the Medium market is held by Powergen, TotalFinaElf and Gaz de France and at least 59 percent of the Interruptible market is held by Powergen, Gaz de France and BP Gas. The next three companies in the Small market are Shell, SSE and BP with 16 percent of the market, in the Medium market BP Gas, British Gas and Shell have 22 percent of the market and in the Interruptible Shell, Statoil and TotalFinaElf have 32 percent. Overall the Top six suppliers are completely dominant (81 percent of the Combined market) and the degree of market concentration measured by the Herfindahl Hirschman Index (HHI) is highest in the Small market and lowest for All Combined. In the Small market the HHI is above the 1880 threshold which UK's Office of Fair Trading views as reflecting a high degree of concentration (OFGEM 2004b: 162). Secondly, from the above, we also know that the Top six companies in any of the market segments are drawn from a pool of just eight companies and seven of these are primarily upstream companies or have upstream interests.

Finally, the significance of the data in Tables 2.9 and 2.10 may be established by referring back to Table 1.1 in Chapter 1, which shows that the non-domestic consumers constituted about 65 percent of the UK market for gas in 2004. From this it may be suggested that the Top six non-domestic supply companies, who together have 81 percent

Table 2.9: Non-domestic Gas Market Share Ranges by Company in 2002

Market Share by Volume	Volume Band (consumption by meter)		
	Up to 50,000 Therms	Over 50,000 Therms	Interruptible
Over 15%	British Gas Powergen/TXU	Powergen/TXU TotalFinaElf	BP Gas Gaz de France Energy
10%-15%	TotalFinaElf	Gaz de France Energy	Powergen/TXU Shell Statoil TotalFinaElf
5%-10%	Shell	BP Gas British Gas Shell Statoil	
Up to 5%	Atlantic Electric & Gas BP Gas Cofathec Heatsave Contract Natural Gas Countrywide Farmers Crown Energy Economy Gas EdF Group ENI UK Fortum Gaz de France Energy Innogy Monal Utilities Norvic Natural Gas Pennine Natural Gas Reepham ScottishPower SSE Statoil Total Energy Gas Supplies V-is-on-Gas	Atlantic Electric & Gas Cinergy Global Trading Cofathec Heatsave Crown Energy EdF Group ENI UK Fortum Innogy Pennine Natural Gas Regent Gas ScottishPower SSE V-is-on Gas	British Gas Cinergy Global Trading EdF Group ENI UK Fortum Innogy SSE V-is-on-Gas
Number of Companies	25	20	14

Source: OFGEM (2003b: Appendix 4, p.79)

Note: Since these data were published Atlantic Electric & Gas has been taken over by Scottish & Southern Electricity (SSE), such that SSE's market share would in all likelihood move up into the next category. Also, in October 2003 Fortum and V-is-on Gas became part of Corona Energy which also absorbed Quantum Energy, Saracen Gas and The Gas Company. In October 2004 BP announced that it is withdrawing from the small-scale end of the industrial/commercial market, focusing on customers who are able to take delivery at NBP.

Table 2.10: Non-domestic Gas Market Shares by Groups of Companies 2002

Market Shares by Volume	Small Market: Below 50,000 Therms	Medium Market: Above 50, 000 Therms	Interruptible Market	Combined Medium + Interruptible	All Combined
Aggregate Share of Top 3 Suppliers	72%	56%	59%	52%	49%
Aggregate Share of Next 3 Suppliers	16%	22%	32%	32%	32%
Aggregate Share of Top 6 Suppliers	88%	78%	91%	84%	81%
Other Suppliers	12%	22%	9%	16%	19%
Herfindahl Hirschman Index	2010	1413	1758	1319	1266

Source: OFGEM (2003b: 47)

of the non-domestic market (Table 2.9), would thereby control about 53 percent of the overall gas market via their non-domestic market activities.

Domestic Market Shares

The data for shares in the domestic market are both more up-to-date and much more straightforward (Figure 2.2). The market is covered by just six major suppliers (British Gas, Powergen, npower, SSE, Scottish Power and EdF) who are in turn dominated by the more than 60 percent share held by the former incumbent, British Gas (Centrica). Such a high level of concentration is reflected in the HHI for this market, which in December 2003 stood at 4049 (OFGEM 2004b: 162) or more than double the level deemed by the Office of Fair Trading as indicative of a highly concentrated market.

Further to this we can note that because the domestic market represented about 35 percent of the overall UK gas market at this time, British Gas (Centrica) thereby controlled about 21 percent of the overall gas market and Powergen about 4 percent by virtue of

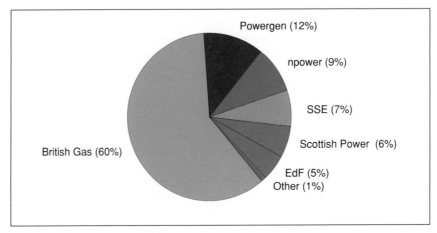

Source: OFGEM (2004b: 157)

Figure 2.2: Domestic Market Shares (Customer Numbers) December 2003

their domestic market activities. These are also the only two companies covering the domestic market which also have a major presence
in the non-domestic market. However, given the form in which the
non-domestic data are presented it is impossible to impute these companies' overall market share by combining domestic and non-domestic
market share data. Instead we can take British Gas' own sales data for
2004 (residential+business sales of c.257TWh – Centrica 2004) which,
combined with the data for the size of the overall market (Table 1.1)
indicates that this company had about 22.6 percent of the overall
gas market. As such, and despite losing 819,000 residential customers
between 2003 and 2004 (Centrica 2004), British Gas must still be the
single largest supplier of final consumers.

Horizontal Integration between Gas and Electricity

Horizontal integration between gas and electricity in the UK is now
almost total in supply and generation.

Non-domestic Supply of Electricity

By shading them in blue Table 2.11 reveals that companies which are
also involved in non-domestic gas supply are dominant in electricity
supply. However, reflecting the fact that they are the former incumbent
electricity suppliers or generators, their dominance of electricity is far

greater than of gas where, as we have seen, upstream gas companies are dominant. Moreover, the non-domestic electricity supply market in general exhibits a higher level of concentration than its equivalent gas market: there are fewer companies and the HHI is respectively almost at or well above the high concentration threshold in the medium and large segments of the market (Table 2.12). Only British Energy offers any competition to the big three, EdF, Innogy (parent RWE) and Powergen (parent E.ON), and it of course has only survived its 2002 financial crisis with government financial assistance. EdF and Innogy,

Table 2.11: Non-domestic Electricity Market Share Ranges by Company, 2002

	Volume Band (consumption by meter)		
	Up to 200MWh	*200MWh to 30,000MWh*	*Over 30,000MWh*
Over 15%	EdF Group	EdF Group	EdF Group
	Innogy	Innogy	Innogy
	Powergen/TXU	Powergen/TXU	
10%-15%	British Gas	British Energy	SSE
5%-10%	SSE	SSE	British Energy
	Scottish Power		Scottish Power
Up to 5%	Atlantic Electric & Gas	Atlantic Electric & Gas	British Gas
	BizzEnergy	British Gas	Smartest Energy
	British Energy	Maverick Energy	TotalFinaElf
	Economy Power	Renewable Energy	
	Fortum	Scottish Power	
	Maverick Energy	TotalFinaElf	
	Renewable Energy		
	Smartest Energy		
	TotalFinaElf		
Number of Companies	15	11	8

Source: OFGEM (2003b: Appendix 4, p.78)

Note: Since the data were published Atlantic Electric & Gas has been taken over by Scottish & Southern Electricity (SSE), such that SSE's market share could now be in the 10−15 percent category.

Table 2.12: Non-domestic Electricity Market Shares by Groups of Companies 2002

Market Shares by Volume	*Small Market: Below 200 MWh*	*Medium Market: 200 MWh to 30,000 MWh*	*Large Market: Over 30,000MWh*	*Combined Medium + Large*	*All Combined*
Aggregate Share of Top 3 Suppliers	57%	65%	81%	67%	64%
Aggregate Share of Next 3 Suppliers	35%	29%	19%	28%	26%
Aggregate Share of Top 6 Suppliers	91%	95%	100%	95%	91%
Other Suppliers	9%	5%	0%	5%	9%
Herfindahl Hirschman Index	1547	1802	3353	1805	1670

Source: OFGEM (2003b: 47)

with at least a 66 percent share, essentially divide up the large market between them.

Domestic Electricity Supply

Compared with non-domestic electricity and gas supply, the position with respect to domestic electricity and gas supply is different only to the extent that the overlap is virtually total – the same six players, EdF, British Gas (Centrica), Innogy (trading as npower), Powergen, Scottish Power and SSE divide up the market between them (Figure 2.3). However, while British Gas emerges as the largest electricity supplier as well as the largest gas supplier, its dominance of the electricity market is well below that of the gas market, such that the HHI, at 1767 in December 2003, was much lower than for domestic gas supply, and also below the danger threshold of 1880 (OFGEM 2004b: 162).

When domestic customer numbers for both gas and electricity are put together, British Gas emerges with a 40 percent share (Figure 2.4). British Gas also has a 44 percent share of the Dual Fuel market (OFGEM 2004b: 161).

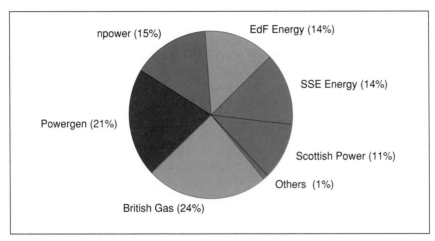

Source: constructed from OFGEM data (2004b: Table 6.1, p. 157)

Figure 2.3: Domestic Electricity Market Shares (Customer Numbers) December 2003

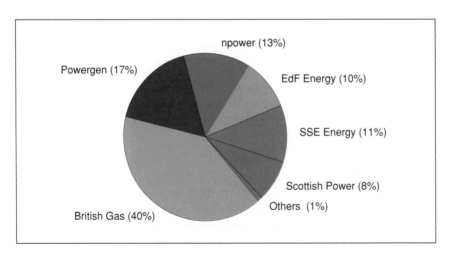

Source: constructed from OFGEM data (2004b: Table 6.9, p. 163)

Figure 2.4: Domestic Gas & Electricity Market Shares (Customer Numbers) December 2003

Generation

Table 1.3 in Chapter 1 already showed us the key gas supply companies with both coal and gas-fired plant (all more of the former), allowing them to arbitrage between gas and coal. Table 2.13 shows the total generating capacity held by both these suppliers and that held by the other main gas and electricity suppliers who also have generating capacity, but no coal-fired plant in their portfolios.

Table 2.13: Electricity Generating Capacity held by Major Gas and Electricity Suppliers

Company	Total Capacity (Mw)	Portfolio Mix
RWE Innogy Plc	8,035	Coal/Gas/Oil/Gasoil/Hydro
PowerGen	7,645	Coal/Gas/Oil/Gasoil/Hydro
EdF Energy	4,823	Coal/Gas/Gasoil
Scottish Power	4,735	Hydro/Coal/Gas/Gasoil
SSE	4,696	Hydro/Gas/Diesel
Centrica	2,174	Gas
TOTAL	32,108	

Notes: **a)** Data for companies other than Centrica as of May 2004, Centrica as of end 2003 **b)** the Centrica (British Gas) capacity data are the net capacity represented by its equity holdings in power plant **c)** for companies other than Centrica the data exclude equity capacity which the companies may hold in gas-fired IPPs. The latter include EdF's and SSE's indirect interests in Barking Power (installed capacity 1,000MW), Powergen's 50 percent interest in Corby Power (753MW) and 26.7 percent interest in Teesside Power (1,875MW), Scottish Power's 100 percent interest in Damhead Creek (792MW) and joint ownership of South Coast Power (400MW).

Sources: DTI (2005a); Centrica (2003).

All of the companies which are present in the non-domestic and domestic gas and electricity markets have substantial generating capacity. Powergen (E.ON) and RWE are the largest generators and together all six companies have about 43 percent of the UK's total operational installed capacity as of May 2004 (73,885MW − DTI 2005a).

The Significance of Company Portfolios

Reflecting now on the ownership of the UK gas chain, the first reaction must be to observe how incredibly complicated it has become after almost twenty years of the downstream joining the private sector. Secondly, it is also clear that some companies have developed or been left with positions of considerable market power – notably Centrica and Shell in Dry gas (swing) production, a small group of companies in the non-domestic market and Centrica again in both storage and domestic gas. However, such a conventional view of market power, expressed in terms of particular markets, really misses the point. Such ownership patterns only reflect potential power – while the real possibilities of using it are constrained by competition law and the fact that its overt flaunting would be difficult to conceal. This does not mean that it will not be used, but even an apparently clear-cut example – Centrica (British Gas), in possession of 44 percent of dual fuel customers, was criticised by OFGEM for consistently, 'offering the most expensive dual fuel price at medium and high consumption levels (in at least 9 out of 14 areas) for direct debit and at all consumption levels (in at least 12 out of 14 areas) for standard credit' (OFGEM 2004b: 161) – actually involves the use of more than one market. This in turn points us towards the importance of portfolios, to the way in which ownership power may actually be used, either without breaking the law or by making it difficult to apply.

Table 2.14 assembles the deployment of company portfolios down the UK gas chain, focusing on those companies which we have identified as the major players. But before proceeding to address this information, it is necessary to contextualise it by first identifying the possibilities which are available for managing gas price risk in the gas chain. These are:

- being an upstream producer
- owning storage
- having an alternative to gas generation
- having a dominant position in a particular gas market
- having interruptible contracts
- having captive domestic consumers
- using the futures market

Leaving aside the futures markets for the moment – here we are concerned with managing price risk by way of owning particular sets of assets – evidence that all of the above are being used is immediately clear from Table 2.14.[7] However, there are distinct differences in

---

7   Because it is a completely new departure, the implications of which are not yet clear, we do not include a discussion of the implications of reintegration into gas distribution – which, for the moment, only affects one of the companies listed in Table 2.14 (SSE).

company strategy. The major companies listed in Table 2.14 broadly sub-divide into those which are managing their risk upstream and those which are managing it downstream. However, there are specific variants on this broad theme. TotalFinaElf, for example, combines a very strong upstream position with a dominant position in the non-domestic market, some presence in the non-domestic electricity market, but no generation capacity or presence in the domestic market. Its upstream position means that it needs neither of the latter. Gaz de France has a relatively weak upstream position and no domestic gas customers, but a strong position in the interruptible gas market. It has no generating capacity, but also no presence in electricity. Centrica has a strong position in the upstream, but this does not eliminate its upstream price risk because, as we saw above, the size of its customer base means that its own production delivers less than half of its requirements. Centrica therefore has a combination of other hedging instruments: a dominant position in the domestic gas market, a strong position in the domestic

Table 2.14: Major Company Portfolios in the UK Gas Chain 2003/4

Company	Upstream UKCS		Offshore Infrastructure		Gas Shipping
	2003 Production (bcm)	% of Dry Gas Production	Major Pipelines	Terminals: % Maximum Daily Flow 2003-04	
BP	13.5	7.1%	SAGE (13.85%),CATS (29.53%), Miller (60%), SEAL (12.375%), Interconnector (10%)	13.1%	Yes
SHELL	10.7	19.4%	Vesterled (4.68%), FLAGS (50%), SAGE (11.39%), SEAL (12.6%), Miller (15%), Fulmar (50%)	26.5%	Yes
STATOIL	0.2	-	Vesterled (20.379%)	none	Yes
TOTALFINAELF	10.8	4.6%	Vesterled (9.038%), CATS (0.57%), SEAL (19.679%), Interconnector (10%)	17.4%	Yes
GAZ de FRANCE	1.5	0.5%	SEAL (5.7%)	none	Yes
CENTRICA (British Gas)	10.9	22.3%	none	11.4%	Yes
EdF	none	none	none	none	Yes
E.ON (Powergen)	0.2	none	SEAL (2.86%)	none	Yes
RWE (npower)	0.2	-	none	none	Yes
SCOTTISH POWER	none	none	none	none	Yes
SSE (see Table 2.7 for Distribution Network Ownership)	none	none	none	none	Yes

Table 2.14: *continued*

Company	Storage Space	Deliverability	Electricity Generation Capacity	Portfolio
BP	none	none	none	none
SHELL	none	none	none	none
STATOIL	none	none	none	none
TOTALFINAELF	none	none	none	none
GAZ de FRANCE	none	none	none	none
CENTRICA (British Gas)	76.2%	21.6%	2,174	Gas
EdF	0.8%	1.4%	4,823	Coal/Gas/Gasoil
E.ON (Powergen)	none	none	7,645	Coal/Gas/Oil/Gasoil/Hydro
RWE (npower)	none	none	8,035	Coal/Gas/Oil/Gasoil/Hydro
SCOTTISH POWER	3.2%	2.6%	4,696	Hydro/Gas/Diesel
SSE (see Table 2.7 for Distribution Network Ownership)	8.8%	9.3%	4,735	Hydro/Coal/Gas/Gasoil

Table 2.14: *continued*

Company	Non-domestic Gas Market Shares			Non-domestic Electricity Market Shares			Domestic Market Shares	
	Small	Medium	Interruptible	Small	Medium	Large	Gas	Electricity
BP	<5%	5-10%	>15%	none	none	none	none	none
SHELL	5-10%	5-10%	10-15%	none	none	none	none	none
STATOIL	<5%	5-10%	10-15%	none	none	none	none	none
TOTALFINAELF	10-15%	>15%	10-15%	<5%	<5%	<5%	none	none
GAZ de FRANCE	<5%	10-15%	>15%	none	none	none	none	none
CENTRICA (British Gas)	>15%	5-10%	<5%	10-15%	<5%	<5%	60%	24%
EdF	<5%	<5%	<5%	>15%	>15%	>15%	5%	14%
E.ON (Powergen)	>15%	>15%	10-15%	>15%	>15%	none	12%	21%
RWE (npower)	>5%	>5%	>5%	>15%	>15%	>15%	9%	15%
SCOTTISH POWER	<5%	<5%	none	5-10%	<5%	5-10%	6%	11%
SSE (see Table 2.7 for Distribution Network Ownership)	5-10%	5-10%	<5%	10-15%	10-15%	10-15%	7%	14%

electricity market, storage, beach swing capacity and generation assets. EdF, RWE, Scottish Power and SSE are more focused on electricity than gas – and they are managing risk with substantial dual fuel generation assets and captive domestic consumers. E.ON (Powergen) has strong positions in both gas and electricity markets and manages risk with the large multi-fuel generation assets, captive domestic customers and a strong position in the interruptible gas market.

How these different portfolios deliver price risk management, may be illustrated with two examples, one from RWE, the other from Centrica. RWE provides us with an example of the way in which captive domestic customers are a useful risk management tool. In its 2002 Report & Accounts, it had this to say about its acquisition of Innogy (npower) during that year:

> On a seven-month basis, the company contributed 379 million Euros in operating results. In the light of the collapse of UK electricity wholesale prices, this is an encouraging performance. Thanks to its strong presence on the end customer market and its flexible, efficient plant portfolio, Innogy was able to offset declines in income in the power plant business. (RWE 2002: 77)

Centrica, in contrast, provides an example of the usefulness of upstream assets:

> Despite a 4 % reduction in production volumes year-on-year, upstream gas profits increased by 7 % to £480 million. The impact of reduced volumes was offset by a 4 % increase in average selling prices and lower operating costs due to the full year effect of the abolition of royalties on offshore gas production net of the additional PRT charge. (Centrica 2003: 8)

Perhaps needless to say, this performance, which contributed 53 percent of Centrica's operating profits, was combined with its captive domestic customer base in managing price risk – high wholesale (i.e. upstream) prices had to be passed on to customers by the British Gas arm of its operations. For British Gas residential it was:

> ... a challenging year for the retail energy industry in Britain with the impacts of warm weather unusually coupled with rises in commodity costs, British Gas increased its turnover by 2.4 % to £6.2 billion (2002: £6.0 billion). This was due to an increase in our electricity market share, higher energy pricing and continued growth in our home services business. (Centrica 2003: 6)

The general conclusion to be drawn from this for the development of our analysis is as follows. If in Chapter 1 we established that supply shocks are more likely and that liberalisation combined with the limited substitutability of demand will translate them into price shocks, in this Chapter we can perceive that the way in which the major company portfolios are held in the gas chain means that supply and price shocks hold no serious fears. They provide opportunities for profit rather than signals to awaken competitive forces. Thus it was that despite losing 819,000 gas customers between 2003 and 2004, the 2004 price rise to which this is attributed also helped British Gas to increase its operating margin on residential energy sales from 2.6 percent to 4.2 percent, thereby raising its profits on this segment of the market by 83 percent from £136 million to £249 million (Centrica 2004: 9).

CHAPTER 3

MARKETPLACES AND CONTRACTS

Introduction

This chapter aims to bring into focus the places or virtual places where gas supply and demand interact in the process of price formation. However, this is not also to say that it is in these market places that prices are *determined*. The thrust of the argument developed in the first two chapters is that price is determined by a wide variety of factors which crystallise as particular deployments of power or powerlessness on the demand and supply sides of the market. Markets are therefore simply places where these deployments are articulated, while contracts govern the way in which they are articulated and are also themselves a reflection of deployments of power.

In referring already to gas markets rather than a singular 'gas market' we are eschewing the simplistic axioms of economic theory. In common with most other markets, 'the UK gas market' is in fact a series of quite different markets, requiring careful empirical examination in order to make sense of their articulation and the process of price formation. Moreover, this examination must take in the institutional and regulatory environment within which they operate and the specific technical characteristics of the commodity and its delivery system, the latter including its contractual forms.

In the case of gas in the UK at the present time, four different markets can be distinguished: the retail market and three different 'wholesale markets': the long-term bi-lateral contract market, the over-the-counter (OTC) market and the on-the-day commodity market (OCM). These markets interact both with each other and with the International Petroleum Exchange futures market (IPE Natural Gas Futures). Moreover, and as we shall see, both the 'long-term contract market' and 'OTC market' could themselves be seen more as containers for a series of different sub-markets (e.g. long-term contracts between the upstream and wholesalers or between upstream companies; OTC Day-ahead, OTC Year-out), although such distinctions might alternatively be seen as a set of different contracts – as the points at which markets and contracts converge.

History

These gas markets did not however simply appear the moment British Gas was privatised in 1986. Moreover, even if they existed (there has always been a retail 'market' for example), their character has been transformed. In 1986 the market was relatively simple and unsophisticated: a virtual continuation of practices which had prevailed under state ownership namely, long-term, often fixed-price contracts between a vertically-integrated monopoly, linked to an initially guaranteed and administratively priced industrial and household market. Competition was supposed to come from competing fuels, a process which was soon frustrated by discriminatory pricing: British Gas' way of competing which led to an early referral to the Monopolies & Mergers Commission in 1988.

The conditions that allowed markets to emerge developed later, throughout the 1990s, and were responsible for fomenting 'gas-on-gas' competition. With respect to the emergence of wholesale markets, there were two key developments. First of all, a review by the Office of Fair Trading in 1991, which followed up on the recommendations of the 1988 Monopolies & Mergers Commission report, proposed that British Gas release contracted gas supplies to its competitors. Secondly, the *Gas (Modification of Therm Limits) Order 1992*, made under the Competition and Services (Utilities) Act of 1992, reduced the threshold for competitive gas supplies from 25,000 therms per annum right down to 2,500 therms per annum, effective from August 1992. These developments, which might be termed 'forced competition', led to the reductions in British Gas' market share found in Table 3.1.

It was then the necessary accompaniment of competition − Third Party Access to British Gas' transportation and distribution system −

Table 3.1: British Gas' Loss of Market Share 1990−1996

Market (excluding Power Stations)	1990	1991	1992	1993	1994	1995	1996
Small firm supply (2,500–25,000 therms/year)	100	100	100	77	52	45	43
Large firm supply (>25,000 therms per year)	93	80	57	32	9	10	19
Interruptible	100	100	100	100	93	57	34
TOTAL (ex. Power Stations)	97	91	81	77	47	35	29
Power Stations	0	9	26	12	17	32	24

Source: OFGAS *Competitive Market Review*

which eventually led to the establishment of the 'On-the-Day Commodity Market' (OCM). Because it could only be by chance that competing third parties would of themselves achieve a balanced gas system, a residual gas balancing function became necessary – in which the OCM was later to have a role to play.

The retail market, as a place where domestic consumers could choose and switch between suppliers, developed in three phases between April 1996 and June 1998 – by which time all domestic consumers were free to choose their suppliers. However, it was not until April 2002 that all price control regulation was lifted from both the gas and electricity domestic markets.

The OTC Markets

Beginnings and Growth

According to the Monopolies & Mergers Commission report of 1993 third party usage of British Gas' pipeline system increased from only four shippers at the end of 1990 to 15 shippers at the end of 1992 (Monopolies & Mergers Commission 1993: Vol 2, p.76). And it was this, according to the IEA (1998), which ignited 'spot' or 'Over-the-Counter' (OTC – see footnote 8, Chapter 1 to refresh the definition), with the first OTC trades taking place in 1992 and the first spot price series being published by Heren Energy in January 1994. Originally, spot transactions were for gas injected at the Bacton entry point on the Norfolk coast, but the standardisation of delivery conditions necessary to underpin an increase in volumes meant that this had to be superseded by National Balancing Point (NBP) trades – and it was, in 1996, although unlike the USA's Henry Hub the UK's NBP was a 'virtual' rather than an actual physical location on the system. Contracts would now be specified in terms of delivery to the new NBP with two consequences. Firstly, prices thereby came to include entry capacity charges. Secondly, gas was liberated from the confines of specific projects and infrastructure routes – how contracted deliveries were sourced would now be a matter for suppliers, eliminating delivery risk for customers. Figure 3.1 shows how volumes traded at the NBP subsequently increased. Moreover, the number and the average size of trade have also increased very substantially: the former starting out at 947 in March 1996 and reaching a peak of over 45,000 in July 2002, the latter up from around 4 GWh in 1996 to as much as 18 GWh in March 2004, before falling back over the following months to April 2005 (Figure 3.2). At the beginning of the period, such NBP trading volumes can be taken as a proxy for OTC volumes. However, as new long-term contracts have been entered into, these have usually been for delivery to NBP – such that daily nominations from

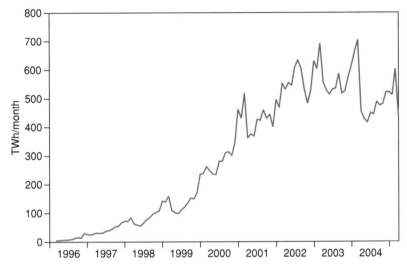

Figure 3.1: Gas Volumes Traded at the National Balancing Point 1996–2005

Source: National Grid Transco (2005)

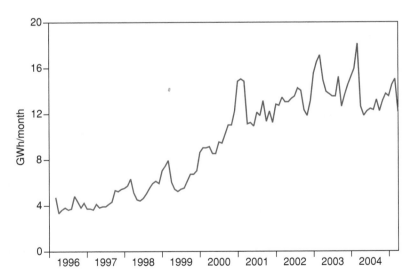

Figure 3.2: Average Size of National Balancing Point Trades 1996–2005

Source: National Grid Transco (2005)

long-term contracts increasingly mix with shorter-term (up to two years' duration) OTC volumes at NBP (subsequently leading us to designate NBP trades as 'NBP/OTC', rather than just 'OTC'). This is also clearly part of an explanation for the increasing average size of trade.

Following on the establishment of an NBP, the next landmark which gave the OTC a more formal presence, was the introduction of a stand-ard contract. Because the OTC is not formally regulated, this was an example of 'self-regulation' and, as such, its exact origins are difficult to pin down. However, it is generally accepted that Enron and BP led the way, with the latter producing what would become an industry-standard contract in 1997 (BP 1997). Because the OTC has no single, identifiable market operator, this contract incorporates the responsibility of market participants to inform Transco about their trades, whether or not there is a firm intention to deliver gas. To be acceptable to Transco buyer and seller nominations must be matched.[1]

Contracts, Trading and Players

Something of the flavour of OTC trading was conveyed by Platts in 2002:

> Over-the-Counter trading (OTC) is one of the most common forms of gas trading. In an OTC deal, two companies conclude a bilateral agreement to buy or sell gas, without the use of an exchange. Such a deal can be carried out directly over a phone between the two parties involved. But many deals are put together by brokers. Using a broker allows a trader to place anonymous bids and offers to the marketplace. Traditional voice brokers work over the phone, but many brokerages now run computer trading platforms that display prices over the internet. Parties involved in OTC trading include a wide range of producers, suppliers, generators and financial traders. (Platts 2002)

To this we can add the following, more detailed characterisations. Firstly, the OTC is not one market but several, distinguished by period of contract moving through Day-ahead, Within-day, Weekend, Working-days-next-week (WDNW), Balance-of-month (BOM), one

---

1 Transco's view of the information which it must receive from OTC traders is expressed somewhat more obliquely as follows: 'Transco are only aware of trades that are carried out via the OCM. Shippers can also trade with each other via other methods, such as the London Clearing House and Spectron. Other than this, shippers have to balance their inputs and outputs on AT-Link (the electronic interface between shippers and Transco). Therefore although we do not necessarily know who a shipper has traded with, we will know their end-of-day position with regards to trade buy and trade sells.' Source: correspondence with Transco

month out, two months out and then various quarters forward. As we have already noted, two years forward is generally considered to be the limit of the OTC market, after which we enter the territory of long-term contracts. Secondly, and reinforcing the character of the OTC as a multiplicity of markets, each market does not engage the attention of the same players. Close to or on the day (Day-ahead, Within-day), all players are involved. Moving forward, only the larger companies are engaged. Thirdly, daily contract volumes generally decrease as the market moves forward. Fourthly, a typical trade is well below the average calculated above: of the 21,762 trades for all contract periods recorded by Heren Energy in 2004 (Heren Energy 2005), only 3010 were for over 100,000 therms per day (2.93 GWh). Fifthly, only a small minority of trades are now bilaterally conducted between party and counterparty − the majority being brokered, an estimated 43 percent via electronic platforms and 57 percent by voice (FSA 2005).[2] Sixthly, while in 2000 there were eleven active brokers, today their number has been reduced to a big three: Spectron, Prebon and ICAP. Seventh, while all upstream producers and suppliers of gas do use the OTC, not all of them actively trade in gas. In particular, and as we already noted in Chapter 2, upstream producers are generally only interested in placing their volumes, not in gains from price speculation. Thus ConocoPhillips, BG plc, Chevron, Marathon Exxon and Perenco either do not trade or trade very little. The main traders are Total, BP and Centrica all of which have both upstream and downstream interests. Centrica is the largest and most consistently active. These three are then joined by the other major suppliers (RWE, E.ON, EdF, Scottish Power and SSE), by banks (Morgan Stanley, Goldman Sachs and Deutsche Bank) and by smaller traders such as Merrill Lynch commodities and Foundation Energy. Finally, forward contracts on the OTC, unlike exchange-traded futures contracts, require no payment until delivery – which means that the buyer bears a performance risk and the seller a credit risk.

Paper Volumes and Physical Volumes

So far, but without making it explicit, we have been describing the growth of the NBP/OTC trades in terms of the growth of all trades which are

---

2   These percentages are derived from the FSA's data for the year to July 2004 which shows 12% of traded gas volumes being traded by exchange, 38% by electronic platform and 50% voice brokered. The exchange-based trading refers exclusively to the International Petroleum Exchange's futures contract (see below), such that we have only used the electronic platform and voice-brokered trades to refer to 100% of brokered OTC trades.

notified to (must be notified to) Transco. This means that we have been using 'paper trade' data, covering all formal exchanges of contract, as opposed to trades which are for physical delivery. The difference between the growth of paper trades and the growth of NBP/OTC trades for physical delivery may be observed in Figure 3.3, growing rapidly such that paper trades came to exceed physical trades by as much as 20 to 1 at peak. This is the so-called 'churn rate' which is an indicator of liquidity and maturity of the market – and which has certainly registered a decline in the wake of the collapse of Enron in December 2001 and the subsequent withdrawal of other US energy traders. However, the churn rate data also need to be treated with caution: the actual and unknowable rate is higher because OTC traders net out their trades with each other prior to notifying Transco of their positions.

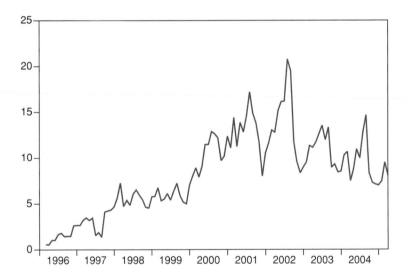

Figure 3.3: Monthly Ratio of NBP Paper Trades to NBP Trades for Physical Delivery, March 1996 to March 2005

Source: National Grid Transco (2005)

Gas Balancing Markets: from Flexibility Mechanism to the OCM

When Third Party Access in the UK became more formally organised in 1996, with the introduction of a 'Network Code' which 'constitutes a contractual agreement between Transco and its customers, known as Users, who utilise the Transco pipe network to transport their gas' (Transco, undated, p.1), there had to be a mechanism whereby Transco could acquire or dispose of gas in order to perform its role of residual system balancer and maintain the physical integrity and safety of the whole pipeline system. Thus came into being the 'Flexibility Mechanism' which, along with 'Daily Gas Balancing', was without precedent in other gas markets throughout the world; and they were developed from first principles through a lengthy period of consultation between OFGAS, BG Transco, gas shippers and other industry participants.

The Flexibility Mechanism operated as follows. If there was a net difference between aggregate shipper inputs of gas and aggregate off-takes from the system during a particular 'gas day' (which ended at 06.00 hours), and which could not be accommodated by variations in pipeline pressure, known as 'linepack',[3] Transco would purchase gas from shippers or sell gas to shippers, in order to preserve the balance. The volume of these purchases and sales of gas were based on prior forecasts of the linepack that would exist at the end of the 'gas day'. The procedures used were called respectively, *System Buy* and *System Sell*, and in fact included a number of measures (such as storage movements and interruption of customer supplies where this was allowable), as well as actual financial transactions. To provide the liquidity for this 'market-based method' (British Gas TransCo 1995: 4) gas shippers (including British Gas Trading) made both 'buy' and 'sell' bids to a screen-based flexibility market whose results were communicated to Transco at 18.00 hours on the day preceding the 'gas day'. During the gas day itself, whenever Transco decided that action was necessary, it would choose the 'best' bid: if Transco required a *System Buy* (to add gas to the system), it selected bids from among those offered in a low-est-to-highest sequence, and in reverse order if a *System Sell* (to take gas off the system) was indicated.

However, in addition, each *individual shipper* was responsible for controlling how much gas it put into the system, and for monitoring its customers' off-takes. These inputs and off-takes were accounted for on a daily basis and calculated on the day following the gas day. Any difference between a shipper's daily input and off-take was bought or sold by Transco in a second financial arrangement known as *Cash-out*.

The terms on which accounts were settled in the Cash-out were

---

3   'Linepack' may be thought of as another form of storage. A target linepack volume was set which varied from day to day depending on demand and other operational requirements (such as temperature change). A tolerance range (known as bandwidth) was defined around this target, also varying with operational requirements.

linked to those arising from the Flexibility Mechanism as follows. For a day on which balancing action had been taken under the mechanism, the *System Average Price* (SAP) was calculated as the weighted average price of all bids.[4] Provided a shipper's imbalance was within a certain tolerance range (on average, about 4 percent of a shipper's throughput of gas) the imbalance was charged or paid at the SAP. However if the imbalance lay outside this tolerance range, the shipper either paid or received the *System Marginal Price* (SMP) for any part of its imbalance outside the range: if the shipper under-delivered he would pay the price of the highest *System Buy* bid selected on the gas day, and if he over-delivered he would receive the value of the lowest *System Sell* bid selected. If no System Buy or System Sell bid had actually been selected during the gas day, the corresponding SMP buy and sell prices were set equal to the SAP. If no balancing action was taken during the gas day, then the SAP (and hence the SMP buy and sell) were set equal to the average SAP on each of the previous seven days.

The charges levied or paid by Transco under the Flexibility Mechanism and Cash-out (together with a third, generally small amount known as the 'Scheduling Charge'[5]) were added together to constitute the 'Neutrality Charge'. The use of this name derived from the fact that Transco's operations in both the Flexibility Mechanism and the Cash-out were intended to leave it cash neutral (i.e. making neither profit nor loss). Therefore each month the total receipts and payments for accepted bids, Cash-out of imbalances and scheduling charges were netted out. Each shipper then received a debit or credit in direct proportion to the amount of gas shipped in that month.

Once the new code began operation certain problems emerged. Firstly, Transco was able to sell unlimited capacity at a fixed price, irrespective of the actual capacity available. Thus, total booked capacity on any day did not necessarily match that which was physically available. Secondly, shippers were able to nominate flows in excess of their booked capacity. In cases where this led Transco to anticipate imbalances in the system it would take remedial action via the flexibility mechanism. The costs of Transco's actions to alleviate the constraints were passed back to companies and ultimately customers. These costs were additional to, not netted off from, Transco's price-controlled transportation charges.

---

4   Excluding any bids selected to address what were known as 'locational constraints' (capacity constraints at particular intake and offtake points).

5   Scheduling charges are payments made by shippers when actual gas flows are different from the companies' final nominations at entry and exit points (a gas flow could be in balance but still different from the nominated amount).

On occasions this would lead to Transco paying exceptionally high prices for relatively marginal amounts of gas, the cost of this action thereafter being transferred to all shippers via the Neutrality Charge. For example, when on December 16, 1997, Transco was forced to carry out three System Buy actions, the first two were at the modest price of around 20p per therm, but the last (for only 2.75 GWh) was at 496.93p per therm. Had the balancing action been taken a few minutes earlier or even for a slightly smaller volume, the SMP price would have been significantly lower. Similar problems on December 17 and knock-on effects in the Within-day market (where shippers try to correct their imbalances by trading between themselves) resulted in total costs of £12 million pounds according to OFGAS (1999:30–1). The problem identified here was essentially that whereas Transco was required to ensure the physical security of the system there was no financial incentive for Transco to do this in a particularly efficient manner.

The latter problem, implying that balancing costs were higher than they need be, was one of a series of problems with the initial gas trading arrangements (between March 1996 and February 1999 there were 315 proposed modifications to the Network Code of which 176 were implemented), which it was felt should be addressed comprehensively rather than piecemeal. This was done via the New Gas Trading Arrangements, introduced in October 1999, part of which was to involve abandonment of the Flexibility Mechanism and its replacement by an On-the-Day Commodity Market (OCM) at arm's length from Transco. While Transco would still retain responsibility for gas balancing and for operating Cash-out along the same lines as before, now System Buy, System Sell and System Average prices would be set according to the prices revealed in a new transparent marketplace. Unlike the Flexibility Mechanism, shippers trading on the OCM would be able to trade with each other as well as with Transco, thereby potentially reducing the need for Transco to intervene.

The OCM

The basic structure and function of the OCM had first been proposed by OFGAS in the summer of 1997. Then in 1999, in anticipation of the introduction of the New Gas Trading Arrangements, a competitive tender to design, operate and maintain the OCM was won by EnMO, a joint venture between the then National Grid (now National Grid Transco) and the US company Altra Energy Technologies. In September of that year, it duly became Europe's first screen-based anonymous

Within-day market for trading wholesale gas. In July 2003 EnMO was acquired by the Dutch APX (Amsterdam Power Exchange) group and in November 2004 was renamed APX Gas. APX Gas is regulated by OFGEM by 'Designation' where the designation criteria relate to Transco's requirements outlined in Section 7 of its Public Gas Transporter Licence. In addition all OCM market participants are subject to regulation by OFGEM through the conditions of their licences issued under primary legislation (the Gas Acts of 1986 and 1995 and the Utilities Act 2000). This form of regulation rather than regulation under the UK's Financial Services Authority (FSA), from which it was granted a special exemption, was decided on the grounds that the OCM is not an *investment* market but a commercial one (defined as a market in which delivery of a contract takes place within seven days). Also the OCM is not a market on which unsophisticated private investors, requiring regulatory protection, are likely to operate.

EnMo's original contract with Transco, covering its first twelve months of operation, guaranteed that Transco would only use the OCM for balancing actions. Since that time, while Transco has the right to use other markets, it has not chosen to do so. One constraint here is that because its trades are used for calculating Cash-out prices, if Transco did choose to use other markets, the prices of these trades would have to be included in the calculation of Cash-out prices. EnMo's current contract with Transco simply passes on relevant regulatory obligations to EnMO. In addition, as a counter-party to all OCM trades EnMo provides Transco with information about the trading position of shippers on a continuous basis. Unlike for OTC trades, Transco accepts this information without the need for matching of buyer and seller and uses it to calculate shipper end-of-day balance positions for Cash-out purposes. The investment cost of establishing the OCM was relatively small, some £500,000 to be recouped from the fees paid by shippers

Three on-the-day-for-the-day products are traded on the OCM in multiples of 100,000 KWh to facilitate gas balancing: Physical gas, Locational gas (linked to particular locations on the transmission and distribution network) and Title gas (a purely paper trade). OCM volumes initially grew dramatically, with winter volumes increasing three-fold from a total of 16 TWh in 1999–2000 to 51 TWh in 2002–03 (Figure 3.4). They then dipped in 2003–04 only to recover sharply in the current gas year, with record volumes being recorded in October 2004 (Figure 3.5). It is difficult to discern a clear seasonal pattern to trading, nor should one necessarily expect to find one given that balancing problems can occur with equal severity during either winter or summer months.

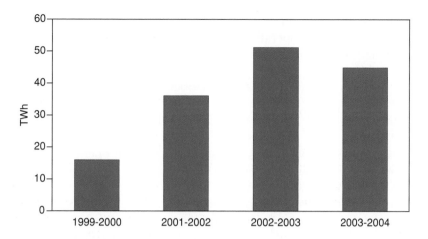

Figure 3.4: OCM Volumes Traded in Winter Periods (October to March)

Source: APX Gas (2005a); OFGEM (2000b)

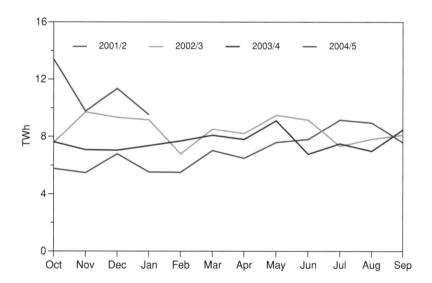

Figure 3.5: OCM Monthly Volumes: 2001/2, 2002/3, 2003/4 and 2004/5 Gas
Years (October to September)

Source: APX Gas (2005a)

Two other trends on the OCM should be noted. Firstly, during its initial months of operation, trading in physical gas ('Physical' or 'Locational') was almost as important as Title gas trading:

Physical gas   (% of market October 1999–May 2000 – **44%**)
Locational gas   (% of market October 1999–May 2000 – **4%**)
Title gas   (% of market October 1999–May 2000 – **52%**)

However since the beginning of its second year of operation, OCM volumes have been virtually entirely Title trades – exchanges of ownership of gas to be shipped which have no effect whatsoever on the volume of gas entering the pipeline system. The implication of this is that the OCM is not itself a vehicle for physically balancing the system – rather, it signals requirements for physical balancing which are then accomplished by way of physical trades on the OTC or by shipper/producers increasing their flows directly.

Secondly, during the first months of operation, Transco was intervening heavily and dominated trading on the OCM (c.45 percent of trades during the first six months). However, this gradually reduced below 10 percent and the data for December 2004 showed Transco's share of trades as 6.86 percent (APX Gas 2005b).

OCM trading now takes place using the EnEx trading platform, to which 55 companies were subscribing as of December 31, 2004 (APX Gas 2005b).[6] Forty-eight of these subscribers were actively trading – the other seven are probably just subscribing for market intelligence reasons (e.g. traders who trade exclusively on the OTC). Twenty-three of the 48 active traders exceeded 5 million therms traded in December 2004 when there were 31 participants on the buy side of the market and 27 on the sell side. However, while the participants on the buy side were relatively evenly weighted, on the sell side one seller held about one-third of volumes sold. This pattern was even more emphatic during the three-month period between September 1 and November 30, 2004 – when one seller had virtually half the sell side (APX Gas 2004).

New Products

During the 2004/05 gas year (starting October 2004) APX Gas has been moving to enter both OTC territory and that of the International Petroleum Exchange's gas futures market (see below) by launching

6   As was recorded in Chapter 2, Table 2.8, by April 2005 the number of OCM members had increased to 58.

Day-ahead, Weekend, Balance-of-the-week (BOW) and Working-days-next-week (WDNW) NBP trading. However, these are only at an embryonic stage with few and sporadic trades for relatively insignificant volumes.

Link-up with Continental Markets

Shortly after the Bacton to Zeebrugge Interconnector opened in 1998, spot trading began on the Continental gas market as it had done in the UK in 1992. Mirroring subsequent developments in the UK, these trades gave rise to the requirement for standard contracts and a hub service. Thus, in October 1999, agreement was reached to establish the Zeebrugge hub, to be operated by Distrigaz, the former Belgian state transmission, distribution and supply company. In November 1999 Distrigaz therefore set up a separate subsidiary company, creatively named 'Huberator', to run Zeebrugge hub trading. Subsequently, as Distrigaz was unbundled during 2001, Huberator became a subsidiary of Fluxys, the unbundled transportation company. In June 2004, APX (Amsterdam Power Exchange – owner of OCM operator EnMO) in partnership with Endex (Dutch-based Energy Derivatives Exchange) signed an agreement with Huberator to open a full-fledged, screen-based Gas Exchange (on-line market and clearing services) at Zeebrugge in January 2005 (APX 2005a).

Trading at the Zeebrugge hub started in mid-2000 and initially grew rapidly. But then in 2003 and 2004, volumes were much reduced (Figure 3.6). Indeed, this kind of erratic liquidity, particularly that of 2003, was noted as a problem by OFGEM in its investigation of the spike in wholesale prices which occurred in October–November 2003 (see Chapter 4). Moreover, this is partly a reflection of some quite fundamental differences between the Zeebrugge hub and the UK OTC. Firstly, there are much fewer trades: less than a fifth of the number recorded by Heren Energy for the UK OTC in 2004. Secondly, trades are generally much larger than in the UK: of the 4,093 trades in 2004, 1,234 were for daily volumes in excess of 100,000 therms. Thirdly, there is generally much less Day-ahead and Within-day trading at the Zeebrugge hub: in January 2003, for example, less than 10 percent of trades by total volume were Day-ahead or Within-day (derived from Heren Energy 2005). The Zeebrugge hub is thus revealed as a much less liquid and less flexible market than the UK OTC – characteristics which have implications for this market's ability to respond to price signals from the UK.

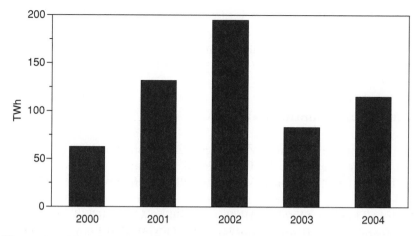

Figure 3.6: Total Trades at the Zeebrugge Hub 2000–2004

Note: This representation of trading growth at the Zeebrugge hub is the sum of all daily trades, whatever the contract period involved. The data for 2000 are from June 1 (trading actually started on May 31).

Source: Heren Energy (2005)

As of July 2005, 43 companies were Huberator customers for trading at the Zeebrugge hub (Huberator 2004); 30 of them are to be found among the members of the UK's OCM (see Table 2.8), the other 11 being Delta, Deutsche Bank, D-Gas, Distrigaz, Dong, EGL, Gasunie, Morgan Stanley, Nuon, SPE, Statkraft, Trianel Energy and ZMB.

Gas Futures

A market in natural gas futures was established by the UK's International Petroleum Exchange (IPE) in 1997, with the first contract being traded on January 31. The market operator is the IPE but The London Clearing House (LCH) acts as a counter-party for all trades, thereby guaranteeing the financial performance of every contract up to and including closure or delivery. The market is regulated by the UK Financial Services Authority (FSA) as a recognised investment exchange (RIE) under Part XVIII of the *Financial Services and Markets Act 2000*.

Five standard gas futures contracts are traded:

1)   'Season': Strip of six consecutive monthly contracts in summer (April–September) and winter (October–March) seasons.

2)   'Quarter': Strip of three consecutive monthly contracts in calendar year quarters (January–February–March etc).

3)   'Month': Strip of consecutive days comprising a calendar month – which may vary in length between 28 and 31 days according to the precise length of the month in question. Monthly contracts are listed for the first 9, 10 or 11 consecutive months of the forward curve.

4)   'Balance of Month' (BOM): contract comprising the number of days remaining in the current month – and which therefore reduces in length each day as the month progresses.

5)   'Day': Day-ahead (D minus 1) to seven days ahead (D minus 7)

All these contracts are 'physical', i.e. they are physically deliverable unless closed out prior to expiry.[7] They are traded in 'lots', each of 1,000 therms per day, with five lots being the minimum contract size. Delivery in contracts above a day in length is in equal portions for each day of the contract.

The growth of the aggregate of IPE Gas Futures contracts volumes is shown in Figure 3.7, along with the growth of by far the most important contract, the 'month out' or 'front month' contract, which

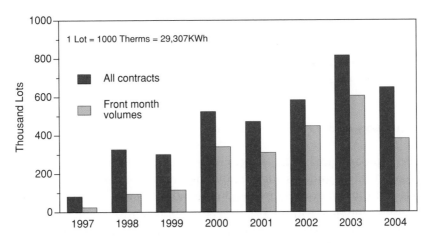

Figure 3.7: The Growth of IPE Gas Futures Volumes 1997–2004

Source: IPE(2005)

---

7   Physical deliverability means that both parties must independently nominate the trade for delivery to Transco via the AT-Link system before 6.30pm on the day prior to delivery.

allows traders to lock into prices on volumes for delivery in the following month. The dip in volumes in 2001 was the result of the arrival of US energy trading companies such as Enron and Dynegy, which boosted OTC trading at the expense of IPE contracts. However the collapse of Enron re-established a sharp upward trend, with IPE front month volumes reaching record levels during 2003. 2004 then saw a dramatic downturn, with front month volumes falling faster than total contract volumes.

The front month contract also provides the basis for the IPE Gas Index price – which takes the rolling arithmetic average of the daily volume-weighted front month price. The importance of IPE Gas Index price is that it has become the 'spot price' upon which 'a large percentage of physical deals are now priced'. (IPE 2003: 17).

The Wholesale Markets Brought Together

Figure 3.8 now provides a representation of how the sizes of the NBP/OTC, OCM, IPE and Beach Contract markets look in relation to each other, and how the scale of paper trades looks in relation to physical trades. Particularly, deliveries to NBP are now greater than those represented by beach contracts and NBP trades for physical delivery are less than 10 percent of total trades (reflecting the 'churn rate'). IPE trades only cover about half of total throughput, while OCM balancing trades are dwarfed by Within-day trading on the OTC. Centrica is responsible for nearly a quarter of throughput.[8]

Contracts and Price Formation

The standard textbooks on economics have, over a number generations, left their students with an abiding impression that nothing comes between the forces of supply and demand and price – textbook prices adjust instantaneously in response to supply and demand, and both then experience feedback from price until an equilibrium position is established. However, as OFGEM's 2004 enquiry into wholesale gas

---

8 This is consistent with the estimate of Centrica's market share made in Chapter 2 (22.6%) – the small difference will be due to the fact that not all gas consumed (the denominator for the calculation in Chapter 2) passes through the national transmission system e.g. five power stations (Peterhead, Teesside, Connah's Quay and two at Killingholme) are 'dual-supplied' (able to take gas directly from offshore as well as from the national transmission system)

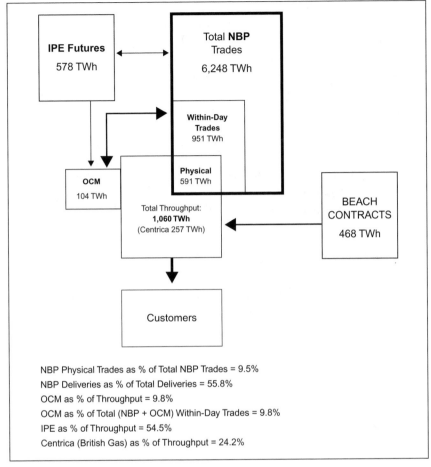

Figure 3.8: UK Market Structure 2004

prices has made it aware, contracts govern the interaction between demand and supply and are likely to frustrate the anticipated outcomes of 'market forces' (OFGEM 2004d: 45). Contracts have two effects on gas price formation. Firstly, they affect the way and the rate at which price signals are transmitted through gas markets towards the final consumer. Secondly, they may themselves be responsible for administering supply-side shocks to the market.

Price Transmission: Contract Length and Pricing

Contract length and pricing have been quite dramatically affected by the liberalisation of the UK gas market. Firstly, while the growth of

NBP/OTC paper trades has been very rapid in relation to NBP/OTC physical trades, this has not prevented the relatively modest growth in the latter from bringing about a dramatic and significant change in the contractual composition of pipeline throughput. This we could already observe in Figure 3.8 which, just for 2004, showed that NBP/OTC traded gas had grown to cover 56 percent of the market, leaving old-style beach contracts in the minority. Figure 3.9 now charts the growth in NBP/OTC-traded gas as a proportion of total pipeline throughput from only 3 percent in March 1996. Figure 3.10 then also charts the declining importance of the old-style beach contracts. However, this development should not be read to imply that 'spot gas' now dominates long-term contract gas in the composition of the UK's gas deliveries. Rather, and as we have already noted, it also reflects the replacement of long-term 'beach' contracts with 'new' long-term contracts which are *for delivery to NBP* (i.e. not linked to a specific source and infrastructure route) and are therefore included in NBP-traded volume data.

Examples of such 'new' long-term contracts for gas imports into the UK which will help make up the shortfall left by declining UKCS gas production are shown in Table 3.2. While these are shorter in length than the 15 to 25 years which typically characterise old-style beach contracts, they are still clearly 'long-term' rather than OTC in nature.

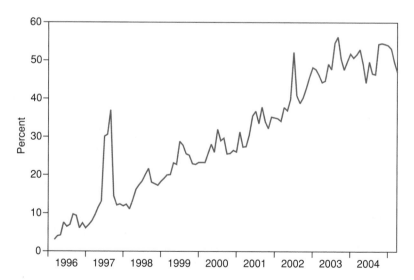

Figure 3.9: Monthly NBP/OTC Physical Volumes as Percentage of Monthly Pipeline Throughput 1996 to 2005

Source: National Grid Transco (2005)

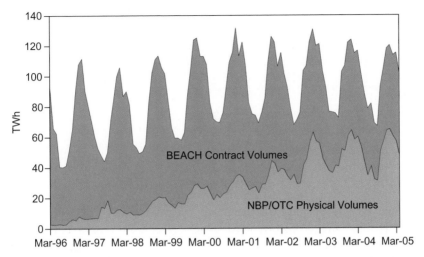

Figure 3.10: Contractual Composition of Monthly Pipeline Throughput 1996 to 2005

Note: NBP/OTC Physical Volumes are superimposed on Total Throughput, such that BEACH Contract volumes are revealed as a residual.

Source: National Grid Transco (2005)

However, the fact that they will usually be at least partially indexed to UK gas market prices, and that they are delivered in daily tranches like any other gas contract, can make them resemble OTC volumes.

Figure 3.11 represents these contractual changes in the UK gas market, moving from the past (showing the contractual options which were used for gas being delivered today) through a present (when gas is being delivered, purchased and sold on the day to resolve imbalances and contracted for the future) to the future (showing the change in the contractual options available today for delivery in the future). The point is that what is shown as the future contractual possibilities in Figure 3.11 are increasingly depicting the past which is structuring the price of today's deliveries. The implications are **a)** that the wholesale price of a larger and larger proportion of the gas consumed in the UK is indexed to or directly priced by short-term markets (in their OTC, OCM and IPE gas futures variants) − by the price of gas which is being actively traded on a daily basis for delivery in the short-term (on the day, next day or next month) and **b)** to the extent that the risks which accompany this transition are marketised (taken to the futures or forward markets), the actual cost of gas today increasingly becomes a weighted average of futures prices from the past, prices which reflect the

Table 3.2: 'New' Long-term Contracts for Gas Imports into the UK

Date	Purchaser	Supplier	Source	Quantity pa	Start Date	Duration	Terms of Delivery	Conditions
Jul-01	BP	STATOIL	Norway via Vesterled pipeline	1.6 bcm	Oct-01	15 years	NBP	conventionally with a minimum take by year end
Jun-02	CENTRICA	STATOIL	Norway: route not specified	5 bcm	Oct-05	10 years	NBP with price linked to UK gas market	conventionally with a minimum take by year end
Jun-02	CENTRICA	GASUNIE	Netherlands via BBL	8 bcm	2006?	10 years	NBP with price linked to UK gas market	swing of 2 bcm between winter and summer months
Oct-03	SHELL + EXXONMOBIL	STATFJORD PARTNERS	Norway via FLAGS pipeline	wet gas in several contracts: total not specified	2007?	10 years	na	na
Under Negotiation	EXXONMOBIL	QATAR PETROLEUM	QATAR LNG	10-20 bcm	2007?	na	'Beach contract' for physical delivery	na

Source: Company information

PAST	OLD LONG-TERM CONTRACTS (Beach Delivery, Oil and Producer Price Indexed)
	MONTHS OUT
	GAS Day minus one (D-1)
TODAY	DELIVERY under PAST CONTRACTS + SPOT PURCHASES and SALES: Within-Day (On-the-Day-for-the-Day): OTC Prompt Desk and OCM. CONTRACTING for FUTURE DELIVERIES: OTC Forward Desk and Bilateral Contracts.
FUTURE UP TO 2 YEARS OUT: OTC FORWARD DESK	SAP-priced (OCM System Average Price)
	MONTH minus one (M-1)
	MEDIUM-TERM CONTRACT (wholly Gas-Indexed)
FUTURE BEYOND 2 YEARS OUT: BILATERAL CONTRACTS	NEW LONG-TERM (NBP Delivery, wholly or partially Gas-Indexed)
	CONTINUING OLD LONG-TERM (Beach Delivery, Oil and Producer Price Indexed)

Figure 3.11: Changing Contractual Structure of the UK Wholesale Gas Market

time profile of the contracts which have delivered gas today. A variant of this understanding was expressed by OFGEM as it puzzled over the relationships between wholesale and retail prices (discussed below in Chapter 6). Referring to electricity prices, but making a point which is equally applicable to gas, OFGEM states, 'Retail prices may not be solely determined by forward prices but may better reflect the weighted average cost of energy (WACOE), which will include not just forward contract prices. In electricity, suppliers will purchase many individual contracts to meet an aggregated demand profile for their customers' (OFGEM 2004b: 91, para 4.41).

Contract Volumes

While OTC trades may be for fixed volumes to be delivered at a specific point in the future, the volumes delivered by long-term contracts can be much less certain. Two basic types of contract are used by the upstream, buyer's option and seller's option (Competition Commission 2003: Appendix 4.6, p.246). Buyer's option, as the name implies, offers much more flexibility to the buyer (a shipper or more usually a shipper/supplier) to respond to changes in the demand for his gas. Buyer's option contracts themselves then come in two versions, depletion (from a specific field) or supply (field source unspecified). Both versions generally involve an annual contract quantity (ACQ) which, in the case of a depletion contract, will be established up to two years before the contract year to reflect the expected performance of the field in question and the buyer's previous takes. However, while some buyer's option contracts may be completely inflexible, more usually within the contract year the buyer has considerable discretion to nominate (24 hours in advance) between a minimum and a maximum take. The latter, expressed as a percentage of the average daily contract quantity (DCQ), quantifies the degree of 'swing' in the contract − which can range from 110 percent to 167 percent (the latter to meet peak winter demand). Minimum takes may vary between 90 percent and zero. If the aggregate of a buyer's daily takes comes in at under a 'minimum bill quantity' (usually 85−100 percent of the ACQ), the buyer will usually still have to pay the minimum bill quantity – thus the term 'take-or-pay' which is applied to such contracts. However, this does not mean that the buyer will have paid for nothing – the quantity not taken will be rolled over to the following year and supplied as 'free gas' once the minimum bill quantity for that year has been taken.

Seller's option contracts are generally depletion contracts and are used with the smaller and more uncertain amounts of gas produced by Associated gas fields. The contract is usually for all the gas that can economically be produced from the field before a specified date. Reflecting the relative unpredictability of Associated gas production, it is not until just before the gas day that the seller makes nominations which the buyer is normally obliged to take.

From the details of these two contractual forms, it can be appreciated how they accommodate the technical uncertainties of UKCS gas production. While both forms harbour uncertainty for the buyer, it is the seller's option contract in particular which may administer supply shocks – as the buyer can have no certainty about the amount of gas which he will have to buy until the last moment. And, as we noted in

Chapter 1, a majority of UKCS gas production now consists of relatively small parcels of Associated gas. The significance of the buyer's option is different: in Chapter 2 we noted that this contract was highly relevant to assessing the power represented by the extent of ownership or operatorship of production. Here we can now state unequivocally that buyer's option contracts tame the market power of UKCS producers of Dry gas. Also bearing in mind that upstream producers, as we also noted in Chapter 2, tend to have an 'engineering outlook' and an economic perspective which is long-term, the possibilities for and incentive to manipulate the market seem in this sense to shift definitively towards the buy-side of the market. But it also needs to be added that such a perspective does not exclude upstream companies from the frame – to the extent that they have independent downstream supply operations and access to privileged upstream information.

The Retail Marketplace

To complete this chapter we come to the retail marketplace, the market which occupies the endpoint in the gas chain. It is also quite different from wholesale markets in having clearly segregated sell and buy sides – retail gas customers do not trade in gas. From Chapter 2 we already know something about the sell side – that the incumbent British Gas still had 61 percent of the market at the end of 2003, and that the rest of the market is divided up between five former incumbent electricity suppliers. Here we add some analytical information about the buy side, about how sellers have been engaging with retail customers since they were all given the opportunity to change supplier in 1998. To do so we draw on OFGEM's most recent *Domestic Competitive Market Review*, published in April 2004.

An important focus of attention for OFGEM is the extent of 'switching' (changing suppliers) among gas and electricity customers – because this is seen as a proxy for the extent to which competitive pressure is being exerted on suppliers. As far as gas is concerned, the outcome so far is that 47 percent of gas customers have switched supplier at least once (gross switching). This compares with 51 percent in electricity. However, because a large number of customers then switched back to the former incumbent, 'net switching' is much lower at 39 percent (the same as in electricity). For example, during 2003, 3.1 million gas customers apparently changed supplier, 42 percent of whom were leaving British Gas and 30 percent rejoining (OFGEM 2004b: 60).

Apart from these indicators of the enduring power of the former incumbent there are a number of others which give more substance to the proposition that retail customers for a homogeneous product are essentially inclined to be 'captive'. Firstly, the rate of switching has been slowing down since the early spurt took net switching to 35 percent by the first quarter of 2002. Secondly, a lower proportion of switchers than non-switchers were satisfied with their gas supplier. Thirdly, between 2001 and 2002, the number of customers expressing no desire to change supplier increased from 18 percent to 28 percent (OFGEM 2004b: 43). Fourthly, the fact that 80 percent of switchers in 2003 took a dual fuel deal (electricity and gas from the same supplier – OFGEM 2004b: 160) is suggestive of a desire for convenience over minimum price discovery. Fifthly, and relatedly, only 65 percent of switchers cited price as the reason for switching supplier, with the other reasons being categorised by OFGEM as 'fixed effects'. And these fixed effects are positively correlated with incumbency in either gas or electricity – with British Gas enjoying by far the highest 'fixed effect' (OFGEM 2004b: 67).

Finally, this last point raises the question of how price signals are conveyed to customers. The answer is very primitively (compared with wholesale markets) and badly (from the point of view of the customer). While wholesale traders in gas can make use of screen-based trading and the market-making price information generated by Heren Energy, retail customers essentially rely on price signals conveyed disparately by individual suppliers and particularly by their doorstep representatives (the largest proportion of switchers got their price information in this way). Moreover, retail customers are atomised and do not have the focused expertise of a trading organisation. Unsurprisingly therefore, in 2003 only 25 percent of retail customers found it very easy to compare gas tariffs between suppliers, down from 33 percent in 2001 – a fall which presumably reflected the rise of dual fuel deals and their adverse effect on price transparency.

CHAPTER 4

WHOLESALE PRICES

Introduction

In this chapter we shall develop an analysis of wholesale prices in four stages. The first stage involves simply describing the trends and measuring the changing volatility of four sets of prices: the Flexibility Mechanism/OCM system prices (Within-day System Average Price, System Marginal Price buy and System Marginal Price sell), UK Over-the-Counter (OTC) prices (Within-day, Day-ahead and Month-ahead), the Zeebrugge hub OTC (Day-ahead differential with UK OTC) and IPE natural gas futures (the benchmark front month and its corresponding 'index'). In all cases we move from the day to the futures. The second stage investigates explanations of the behaviour of these price series: introducing the role of demand, the impact of gas balancing and the analysis of price spikes developed by OFGEM during its 2004 probe into wholesale prices. The third stage involves looking at the relationships between the different gas price series, and then examining their potential and actual behavioural links with oil, coal and electricity prices. Finally, we produce some price formation typologies in order to illustrate the different interactions of the key factors responsible for wholesale price formation.

But before setting out to grapple with the data, it is worth spending a moment discussing their nature and significance. This is because all of the price series which we shall encounter are in effect samples – none of them in any sense capture the whole market or 'the price of gas', they are revealed in different ways and some prices are not revealed at all (unbrokered bilateral OTC trades which may account for as much as 15 percent of the market by volume). Of the prices which are revealed, OCM prices are transparently revealed via an electronic trading exchange and only directly price a relatively small proportion of the market (refer back to Figure 3.8 in Chapter 3). OTC prices directly price a much larger volume of gas and may also be revealed via transparent trading platforms such as that of Spectron, whose prices are independently validated and published by Deloitte Touche. However, in large part (perhaps 50 percent of volume traded) OTC prices are revealed to independent energy information organisations which publish an average of these reports while maintaining the anonymity of their sources. For UK gas Heren Energy is absolutely dominant as the most consistent, reliable and respected publisher of OTC prices. Lastly, futures prices: as an exchange-traded product these are by definition completely transparent and, according to the Financial Services Authority (FSA 2005), took a 12 percent share of the market in the year to July 2004.

The latter should not however suggest that the significance of a particular price series may be gauged by reference to the quantities of gas traded which it directly prices. Three problems, which we shall have to engage with, interfere with this conclusion. First of all, and as we have seen, the amount of gas traded is quite different from the amount of gas dispatched and sold each day – and it is the relationship between the pricing of trades and the pricing of deliveries which will determine the importance of a particular price series. Secondly, and relatedly, while the amount of gas that is bought and sold on a short-term basis only constitutes a part of actual deliveries (the residual left by the volume of long-term contracts), because of the changing nature of long-term contracts, these prices may be wholly or in part determining the delivery price of long-term contract volumes. This happens most explicitly via the use of the main gas price indices (e.g. the Heren Day-ahead and Forward Month indices and the IPE Index (front month) to price gas on the day of delivery. But even this process is not as clear-cut as it seems because the monthly indices are in fact rolling averages of the month to date, thereby smoothing out daily variations, while even the daily prices may obscure influential within-day dramas. Thirdly, there is the question of the relationship between the different price series – between the OCM and the OTC and between the OTC and the IPE. Does one of these series move the others? If so, which and how? Trying to answer this question is to look for the how as well as the why part of price formation, including the possibility that the how of price transmission may be important to understanding the why of price formation. The implication of all these preliminary considerations is that the concept of a 'spot market' or a 'spot price' for gas has already become irretrievably blurred.

Flexibility Mechanism and OCM Prices

Figure 4.1 shows the evolution of the System Average Price from its inception when the Flexibility Mechanism was introduced, through the introduction of the OCM in October 1999 to early 2005.

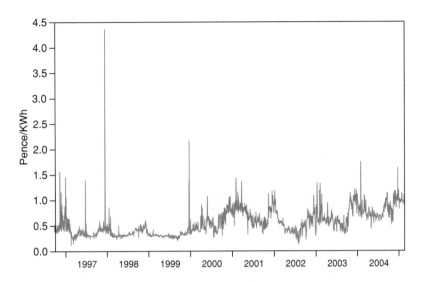

Figure 4.1: Daily System Average Price (SAP) October 1996 to February 2005

Sources: National Grid Transco (2005); APX Gas (2005a)

It reveals a turbulent start to the Flexibility Mechanism, followed by relative calm interspersed with a couple of dramatic price spikes. The OCM then makes a turbulent start and calms down, but generally produces a more volatile pattern of prices than the Flexibility Mechanism. From August 2002, prices are on a rising trend. Figure 4.2 measures the pattern of volatility more precisely using the standard deviation of the daily price changes during each successive gas year. While the System Sell and System Buy prices for Cash-out purposes under the gas balancing regime, respectively System Marginal Price (SMP) Sell and SMP Buy, are less important from our point of view because they only affect the price of a small quantity of imbalance supplies each day, the contrast with the SAP is worth making (Figures 4.3 and 4.4).

It shows, as one might expect, greater extremes of volatility for SMP Sell and SMP Buy, the former under the Flexibility Mechanism and the latter during the first year of operation of the OCM. From 2000, however, the volatility of both SMP Sell and Buy appear a little more settled year on year than the overall SAP – although the level of volatility is generally higher, particularly for SMP Sell. All three series show no evidence of any secular increase in volatility.

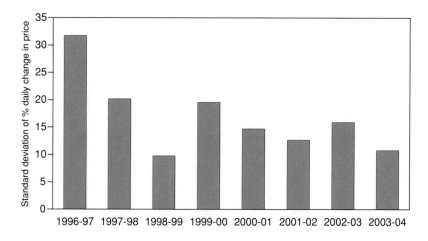

Figure 4.2: Volatility of the System Average Price (SAP) 1996−2004
(in 'Gas Years' – October to September)

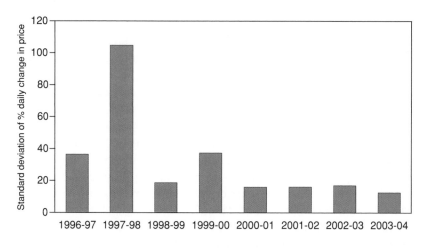

Figure 4.3: Volatility of the System Marginal Price Sell (SMP Sell) 1996−2004
(in 'Gas Years' – October to September)

Sources: data from National Grid Transco (2005) and APX Gas (2005a)

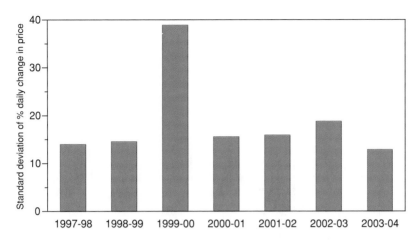

Figure 4.4: Volatility of the System Marginal Price Buy (SMP Buy) 1996–2004 (in 'Gas Years' – October to September)

Sources: data from National Grid Transco (2005) and APX Gas (2005a)

OTC Prices

Within-day

Figure 4.5 shows the evolution of OTC 'Within-day' (on-the-day-for-the-day) gas prices as reported to Heren Energy. These prices are the OTC equivalent of the OCM System Average Price (SAP), and their history shows a similar pattern: volatility increasing after the introduction of the OCM, a rising trend since August 2002 and, while there have clearly been dramatic instances of extreme volatility, no secular increase in volatility can be observed (Figure 4.6). Indeed, the pattern of volatility observed for OTC Within-day prices is similar in trend, extent and level to that of the OCM SAP.

Day-ahead

The trend in OTC Day-ahead prices is shown in Figure 4.7 and their volatility in Figure 4.8. As a forward price, albeit one very close to the day, one might expect it to exhibit less volatility than OTC Within-day or the SAP because there is still time to remedy problems. However, the picture that emerges is more ambiguous. Firstly, in five out of the six years for which we have data, Day-ahead volatility has generally been below that of Within-day. Secondly, and on the other hand, Day-ahead

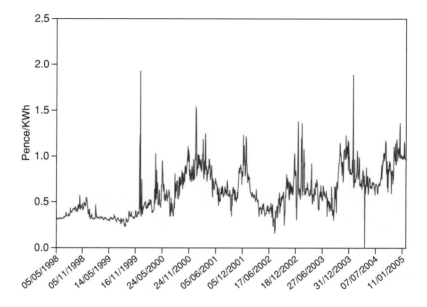

Figure 4.5: OTC Within-day Prices May 1998 to February 2005

Source: Heren Energy (2005)

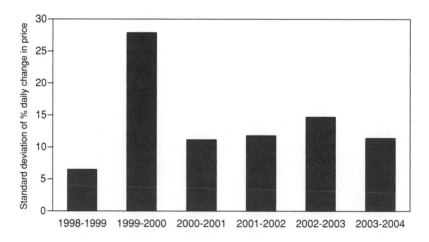

Figure 4.6: Volatility of Within-day OTC Prices 1998–2004 (in 'Gas Years'
– October to September)

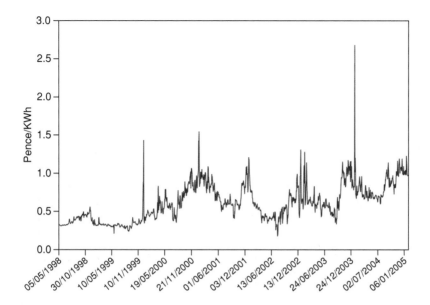

Figure 4.7: OTC Day-ahead Prices May 1998 to February 2005

Source: Heren Energy (2005)

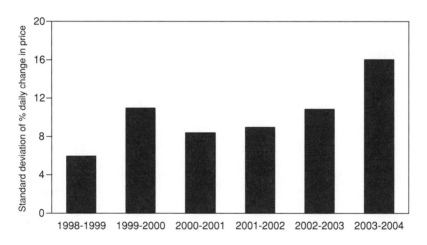

Figure 4.8: Volatility of Day-ahead OTC Prices 1998–2004 (in 'Gas Years'
– October to September)

volatility appears to be on a rising trend. Thirdly, the latter is in general deceptive because it has been triggered by a relatively small number of extreme events – on January 23, 2004, for example, an extreme price swing is readily observable in Figure 4.7 which, if it is removed, reduces 2003–04 volatility below that of the previous gas year.

Month-ahead

The Month-ahead prices in Figures 4.9 and 4.10 are, like the Within-day and Day-ahead series referred to as an 'Index'. This is because they are volume weighted averages of the prices during the period under consideration. In the case of the Heren Monthly Index presented in Figure 4.9 this is calculated as a volume weighted average of the daily prices of the front month contract in the month preceding that month. Thus the monthly index price for e.g. April 1995 is the average of the April forward price from the preceding month. While, like the prompter price indices, the Heren Monthly Index has been on a rising trend since August 2002, it also clearly illustrates the impact of the opening of the Interconnector in 1998 – prices clearly shift out of a comfortable seasonal mode onto both a higher plane and one which has been exhibiting increasing volatility.

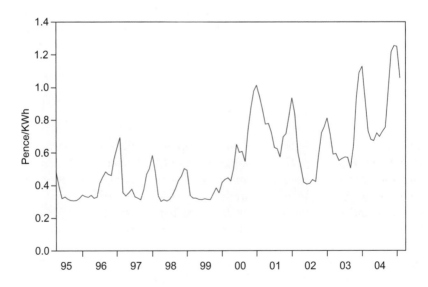

Figure 4.9: OTC Month-ahead Prices April 1995 to February 2005

Source: Heren Energy (2005)

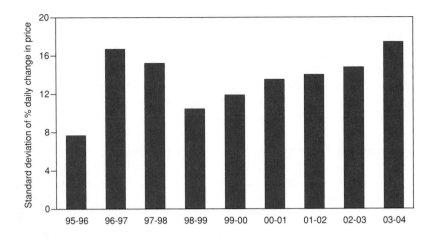

Figure 4.10: Volatility of Month-ahead OTC Prices 1995–2004 (in 'Gas Years'
– October to September)

With respect to the latter, Figure 4.10 shows that the volatility of the
Heren Monthly Index is high and has been rising steadily since 1998,
before which a lack of liquidity in a new market probably produced
the observed high rates of volatility. However, unlike the Within-day
and Day-ahead series, the volatility of the Month-ahead series is with
respect to a recurring seasonal pattern rather than being a function of
a limited number of actual or predicted extreme events – it is telling
us that seasonal variations in price are becoming more extreme.

IPE Natural Gas Futures

This last point has also been picked up in a study of International
Petroleum Exchange (IPE) futures by Energy Markets Ltd (2004: 9),
and they ascribe it to a combination of a perceived shortage in peak
gas/storage/tradable gas (limiting the scope for arbitrage between
summer and winter) and the lack of market makers (a role previously
filled by Enron and Dynegy). The IPE's front month Index is however
different from the Heren Index. First of all, it is of course a futures
rather than a forward index because IPE contracts are exchange-traded.
Secondly however, the methodology used to construct it is different from
the Heren Index – it is calculated as an unweighted rolling average
of the volume-weighted settlement price during the last 15 minutes
of each trading day. The final index for each month is then taken on

the calendar day that the front month contract expires (the last but one business day in each month) and, like the Heren Index, is then published at the beginning of the front month in question. Because of this difference in methodology we therefore chose not to use the IPE Index in our analysis here, but rather the weighted average daily price (Figure 4.11). Later on, however, we shall compare the behaviour of the Heren and the IPE Monthly Indices.

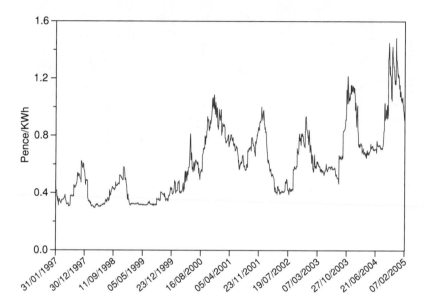

Figure 4.11: IPE Daily Trade-weighted Front Month Futures Prices

Source: IPE (2005)

Figure 4.11 shows us that, like Month-ahead OTC prices, IPE front month futures prices have been on a rising trend since mid-2002. However, the daily volatility of this series (Figure 4.12) is both much lower and more stable than the volatility of the SAP, OTC Within-day and OTC Day-ahead. Here again, a finding by Energy Markets Ltd opens the door to an explanation – they found that the volume of trades has been migrating towards the near term. Between 1997 and 2000 about 20 percent of Open Interest was accounted for by the front month and 50 percent by the first four months. But by 2003, 40 percent of Open Interest was for the front month and 80 percent for the first four months (Energy Markets Ltd 2004: 6). The liquidity of the front month market has therefore been increasing dramatically relative to far out months, a development which, in a transparent market, is of course compatible with much lower levels of volatility.

For this same reason, Energy Markets found the forward curve to be an unreliable indicator of the actual prices that would eventually be paid for gas. The lack of liquidity in longer-term trading has produced a situation in which futures prices have been consistently on the upside of the final price – rather than reflecting the expected equal probability of being upside or downside.

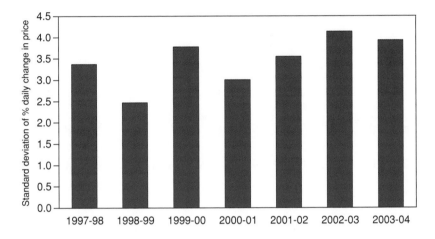

Figure 4.12: Volatility of IPE Front Month Futures Prices 1995–2004 (in 'Gas Years' – October to September)

Zeebrugge Hub Differentials

The Zeebrugge hub links the UK short-term markets with continental short-term markets and the extent to which these marketplaces are synchronised is measured by the Zeebrugge-NBP Day-ahead differentials shown in Figure 4.13. The fact that they are not well-synchronised and indeed show very large differentials at particular times, reflects fundamental differences in the way gas is sourced and contracted for in the two markets, and the way it is delivered between them. On the one hand, continental winter demand for gas is met not from beach-swing but from storage – and storage has to be filled in advance during the summer months. Coupled with contracts which are oil-indexed, a positive Zeebrugge differential may therefore develop during the summer and autumn, as it did in 2002 and 2003. On the other hand, supply-side problems in the UK have opened up large and sudden positive

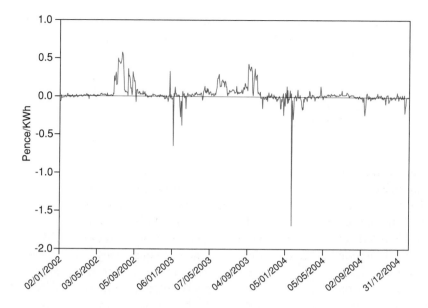

Figure 4.13: Zeebrugge NBP Spread on Day-ahead Indices 2/1/02 to 4/2/05

Source: Heren Energy (2005)

NBP differentials to which supply cannot quickly respond because of infrastructure constraints: the Interconnector is in export mode and may only reverse flow with a lag both for technical reasons and because the timing may be such that a UK supply shortfall coincides with storage replenishment on the continent. Moreover, the fact that the two markets appear to be somewhat better synchronised as 2004 progressed only disguises the fact that oil prices were generally pulling both series up in tandem. All of these factors and the interactions between them will now be considered in much more detail as we begin to analyse wholesale price formation.

Price, Cost and Demand

Moving now to consider explanations for the behaviour of wholesale gas prices, cost and demand form part of conventional explanations. Whether or not upstream gas producers can be considered price-takers in exactly the same way that they are with respect to oil, the pattern of gas price movements which we have just discussed indicates that wholesale gas price formation has no connection with cost plus. In any event, cost of production is a difficult concept to apply in the case of gas because of large sunk costs and the fact that the cost of associated gas production is difficult and not particularly useful to estimate. Moreover, any indirect influence on price via production will only make itself felt via variations in planned increases in capacity, rather than via current production.

As far as the influence of demand is concerned, whether a relationship between demand and price may now be more formally investigated is a more difficult question than it might at first seem. As we have seen, while gas demand materialises in its entirety on the day, Within-day price formation only covers a fraction of gas demand – most gas demand on the day has been met at a price determined before the day in anticipation of the level of demand on the day. A suitable proxy for demand under these circumstances might be considered to be the level of demand which appertains to a particular market e.g. Within-day market demand. But this would in fact be to use the volume of trading in a particular market – which is not the same as the physical volume of gas demand. Despite these problems, it is worth attempting to form some general impression of the relationship between demand and price. This is done in two ways. First of all, we conduct correlation and linear regression tests on the relationship between daily UK system demand and the Flexibility Mechanism/OCM System Average Price (SAP) for the whole of the period that an SAP has been available (from October 1996 to January 2005). The resulting correlation coefficient comes out relatively weak at 0.49, while linear regressions with demand as an independent variable produce an indication that the influence of demand over price is only minor.[1]

Secondly, we also examine this relationship during a particularly momentous gas year (2003–04) which embraced both the escalations in wholesale prices investigated by OFGEM (to be discussed below in greater detail). The latter can be studied in Figure 4.14 where it is already particularly striking how the August/September 2004 price escalation takes off in a way that is evidently completely unrelated to the level of demand. Unsurprisingly therefore, tests on this particular gas year reveal a lower degree of correlation than for October 1996 to January 2005 and the influence of demand over price is shown to be either very weak or negative. Moreover, even the very weak relationship is misleading because on days such as January 29, 2004, when demand

---

1   Because the statistical tests used here and subsequently in the book are standard output from a software package and are used in a supporting role, the details are not included. However, any reader wishing to have these tests confirmed in detail need only apply to the author.

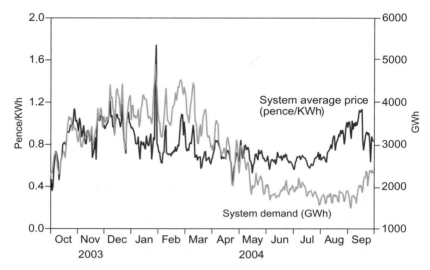

Figure 4.14: Price and UK Daily System Demand during Gas Year 2003−04

Note: UK system demand is total system demand net of Interconnector export nominations

Sources: APX(2005a); National Grid Transco (2005)

appears to be pulling prices dramatically upwards, the real cause was offshore field failures which forced Transco into the market to buy. Also, at the end of the preceding week a fault had closed the Rough storage field for four days, forcing it to declare force majeure and unsettling prices (OFGEM 2004h: 28−29; Farrington 2004). We can therefore conclude that, even if the relationship between demand and price is considered conceptually safe to test, demand has not played a significant independent role in wholesale gas price formation.

Within-day Prices: Liberalisation and Gas Balancing

As we suggested in Chapter 1 volatile prices are to be anticipated in the context of liberalisation: as gas chain relationships become increasingly marketised so prices become highly sensitive to relatively minor supply and demand imbalances and to the behaviour of an increasing number of players with increasingly complex participations and interactions in the chain. An important and highly specific example of such marketisation is the use of a market to facilitate gas balancing, something which, as we have seen, has been associated with price changes showing a standard deviation in excess of 10 percentage points (Figure 4.2).

In the previous chapter we provided some background to the gas balancing problems which are associated with liberalisation – taking us up to the point at which the OCM was introduced under the New Gas Trading arrangements of September 1999. Here we take the story forward in order to bring into focus the problems which have beset gas balancing more recently, and how these have been related to price formation.

Profiling, Regulatory Incentives and Price Volatility

As the OCM opened for business two other important changes were made to the balancing regime. Firstly, there was a sharpening in the incentive to shippers to achieve an end-of-day balance as the imbalance tolerance allowed to shippers before they faced Cash-out penalties was reduced by 25 percent. Secondly, as part of Transco's System Operator (SO) incentive scheme, a financial incentive/penalty was introduced to encourage Transco to minimise balancing costs by trading close to the System Average Price.

However, these measures only marked the beginning of an almost continuous regulatory review extending to April 2003.[2] The key issue to emerge was the problem of shipper 'profiling' gas inputs into the National Transmission system – failure to deliver according to demand and nominations during the early part of the gas day which was having two major effects. Firstly, a potentially dangerous security of supply problem as under-delivery caused linepack to deteriorate. Secondly, this deterioration in linepack prompted Transco to intervene on the OCM in ways that provoked high and volatile prices. Figure 4.15 illustrates this problem.

On the other hand, while profiling could be demonstrated to exist and be causing significant disturbances, it was proving more difficult to ascertain who was responsible. Shippers were initially blamed: their shippers' licences obliged them to flow gas on a 1/24 basis i.e. at a uniform rate throughout the day. But then it was impossible to link particular individual shippers with particular events. Moreover, there was also the possibility that shippers were not to blame or at least not wholly to blame if physical gas inputs were not responding to shipper nominations, i.e. if flow rates were being influenced by problems upstream. And, even if shippers were to blame OFGEM was not able to identify 'whether this was a legitimate response to shippers closing out positions on the day or whether it was an attempt to force Transco

---

2   see OFGEM (2000a, 2000b, 2001a, 2002a, 2003a).

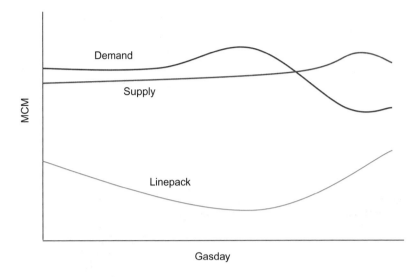

Figure 4.15: Within-day Supply Profiling and its Effect on Linepack

Source: based on OFGEM (2002a: Vol 1, Figure 3.6, p.20 – recording profiling
       and its consequences on November 9, 2001)

to take balancing actions on the other side of the market' (OFGEM
2002a: Vol 1, p.33).

OFGEM and Transco responded in June 2001 by introducing a
'linepack incentive' aimed at reducing the variation between opening
and end-of-day linepack. Transco, it was hoped, would no longer focus
exclusively on responding to its price incentive at the expense of end-of-
day deteriorations in linepack.[3] However, it was later to be shown that
Transco was simply able to offset its losses on the linepack incentive
with gains from the price incentive. Moreover, it was suggested that
in pursuit of its price incentive Transco was delaying its interventions
until late in the day (when the end-of-day SAP would be more readily
predictable) – thereby actually itself being the cause of significant
Within-day linepack swings (OFGEM 2003: 22).

The result was a complex interaction of shipper behaviour and
Transco responses to regulatory incentives. Relating this to price behaviour, the key sequence of relationships is depicted in Figure 4.16.
However, while OFGEM found in its February 2002 Review (OFGEM
2002a) that the bout of extreme OCM price volatility on November
9, 2001 could be linked with Transco interventions explicable in the

---

3   Network Code modification 414 'Proposal to reform the Transco incentive
    redesign'

context of Figure 4.16, analysis of a previous case (March–June 2000) had not arrived at the same conclusion (OFGEM 2000b: 91). Here we therefore conduct a further test using the month of October 2003 when a tremendous spike in the SAP, which more than doubled from 0.4679p/KWh on October 11 to 1.1444 p/KWh on October 28, prompted the OFGEM enquiry which we shall discuss below.

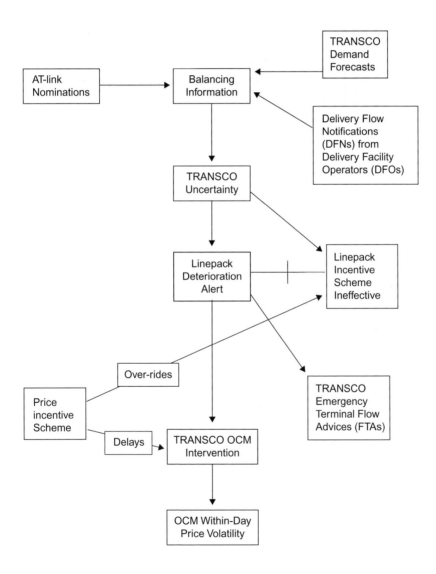

Figure 4.16   Factors Affecting Gas Balancing

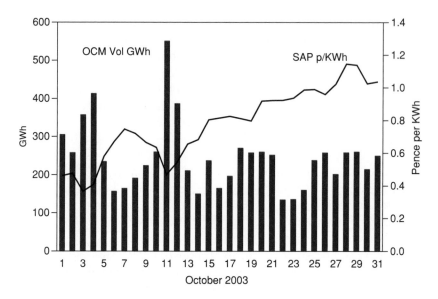

Figure 4.17: OCM Volumes and the System Average Price − October 2003

Source: APX Gas (2005a)

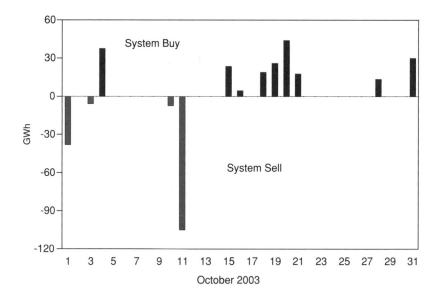

Figure 4.18: Transco System Buy and System Sell − October 2003

Source: National Grid Transco (2005)

The test has two lines of enquiry: to discover whether there was any relationship between the daily volumes traded on the OCM and movements in the SAP (Figure 4.17) and to discover whether Transco's own pattern of trading could have been the cause (Figure 4.18).

Considering the relationship between the sharp increase in the SAP and the volume of trades in Figure 4.17, it is immediately evident that there was no relationship between the two. Figure 4.18 shows Transco's daily balancing actions on both sides of the market and although there is some suggestion of a 'bunching' of buy actions between the 15th and 21st days of the month, it seems unlikely that this could have had much influence on prices since the volumes themselves are historically quite small. Indeed, as we saw in Chapter 3, shipper-to-shipper trades were by this time dwarfing the volume of Transco actions which had fallen below 10 percent of the market.

Being thus unable to replicate OFGEM's 2002 finding of a link between gas balancing problems and extreme movements in the SAP does not mean that gas balancing problems may not be influential in price formation from time to time. However, it does mean that we have to look at factors which may be driving the OCM from the outside.

Such a quest raises the curtain on OFGEM's investigation of the extreme wholesale price volatility seen not only in October but also in November 2003 and then again in August and September 2004. These dramatic escalations in price produced a loud clamour for an enquiry particularly because, on the surface of things, those adversely affected felt that there were no readily apparent reasons why prices should have risen so sharply and suddenly. The result was a two-part OFGEM investigation: an Interim report investigating the wholesale price spikes of October and November 2003 (OFGEM 2003a) and then a follow-up report (OFGEM 2004d) with detailed Appendices (OFGEM 2004e) which also took in the even more dramatic price spikes of August and September 2004. These reports, and particularly the Appendices, provide fascinating raw material and a unique insight into the way the UK gas market works in practice − which we can use to good effect to approach an understanding of gas price formation in the UK.

Explaining Price Shocks: OFGEM's Probe

October−November 2003

OFGEM's approach is notable for its common sense and rigour as it methodically searches for culprits, unpicking the possibilities layer by layer. The starting point is to list the possible explanations for the 18 pence per therm increase in prices and their persistence at the resulting historically high levels through October and November 2003. These are (OFGEM 2004a: 13–16):

- changes in the composition of supply (lower beach supplies, sourcing via the Bacton-Zeebrugge Interconnector, use of storage)
- higher levels of demand
- within-day manipulation of 'linepack' ('profiling' in the parlance of our preceding discussion of the impact of gas balancing on price formation)
- price movements in linked commodity markets (oil, electricity and coal)
- manipulation of markets
- decrease in market liquidity
- market sentiment

All of these factors apart from two are dismissed as either not having played a role (e.g. demand was little different from the preceding year and, as we have just confirmed, gas balancing problems could not be held accountable), or having been a consequence rather than a cause (e.g. unseasonal draw-downs on storage). The two explanations which did emerge centre stage were curtailments in beach supplies (compared with October and November 2002) and the apparent failure of the Interconnector to respond to market signals. The former was particularly apparent at five coastal sub-terminals: St Fergus-Shell (down over 50 percent in both October and November), Bacton Perenco (down 19 percent in October and 21 percent in November), Bacton-Tullow (down 23 percent in October and 31 percent in November), Bacton-Shell (down 3 percent in October and 16 percent in November) and Teesside-BP (down 25 percent in October and 4 percent in November). Such curtailments clearly had serious implications given that, as we saw in Chapter 2, these sub-terminals together deliver about a third of UK beach supplies (Table 2.4).

The Interconnector signalled its potential culpability because shippers had apparently behaved perversely: as NBP prices rose relative to Zeebrugge Troll prices they continued to nominate export flows for the three weeks between October 15 and November 4, such that the Interconnector remained in export mode during this period (OFGEM 2004a: Figure 4.13, p.32). Was the market being ignored or manipulated?

Both of these potential causes of the October–November price spike required the further information and analysis which five months later were provided by OFGEM's second and concluding report and its appendices. Its significance to understanding price formation makes it worth conveying in detail, particularly because nobody turns out to be demonstrably guilty.

Beach Supplies

Here the contentions to be investigated further were the claims of producers that the curtailment of beach supplies at the five key sub-terminals in October and November 2003 was the combined result of planned and unplanned maintenance plus the depletion of certain UKCS fields. OFGEM's findings were, first of all, that depletion did play a role – as our aggregate data showing a secular decline in beach supplies suggest it might have done (Chapter 1, Figure 1.6). In the case of the particular sub-terminals under investigation the larger fields feeding them such as Alwyn, Brent, Britannia, Bruce and Shearwater were shown to be in secular decline. Moreover, the development of new field supplies to replace them had been slipping (OFGEM 2004e: 4). However, even though the depletion effect reduced year-on-year availability by an estimated 18 percent (OFGEM 2004e: Figure a1.3, p.7), surely this problem was more or less predictable and not capable in itself of delivering sharp supply-side shocks? Moreover, can a depletion effect really be distinguished from the generally less predictable flows of Associated gas compared with Dry gas, reinforced by seller-nominated contracts? With respect to the latter, OFGEM later asserts that UKCS Associated gas is being produced at maximum capacity, reinforced by the stimulus to oil production provided by high oil prices (OFGEM 2004e: 87–8), but evidence to support this assertion is lacking. We shall return to this issue below in the context of discussing the relationship between oil and gas prices.

In any event for OFGEM the onus therefore shifts to maintenance – and indeed it was discovered that unplanned maintenance was a serious issue, reducing beach supplies at the five sub-terminals by an estimated 11 percent. Adding this to the 7 percent reduction accounted for by planned maintenance produces a substantial reduction in beach supplies for October and November 2003 which, if it had not occurred (i.e. if all maintenance-affected supplies had been available), would have allowed UK gas supply and demand to have been more or less in balance during the affected months. However, this discovery does not identify a culprit both because there are no historical data to indicate whether the observed pattern of maintenance was particularly unusual, and because all of the producers concerned were able to provide OFGEM with information which in all cases it found to be acceptable demonstrations that all the maintenance was necessary and carried out in a timely fashion (OFGEM 2004e: para 1.2, p.8). Amongst the problems which producers had had to contend with were unplanned outages at the Brent complex and the Gannet field (affecting flows at the St Fergus-Shell sub-terminal), a severe hydraulic fault of several weeks' duration at the Sean field (affecting flows at the Bacton-Shell sub-terminal), a compressor shut-down at the Bacton-Tullow sub-terminal (which led field operators to overreact in adjusting their production plans) and required maintenance at the Armada, Seymour and J-Block fields (affecting flows at the Teesside BP Amoco sub-terminal).

If the untimely maintenance of the UK's ageing offshore infrastructure provides the main explanation of the October–November supply-side shock, OFGEM did also discover a more minor but nevertheless very interesting contributory factor: it estimated that some 4 percent of the reduction in supplies at the five sub-terminals was due to 'contractual constraints' which meant that gas which was physically available to help alleviate the supply shortage was not in fact made available. These constraints were associated with Dry gas, buyer-nominated contracts and affected deliveries to the Bacton-Tullow and Bacton-Shell sub-terminals. They are interesting because although Centrica was involved as the main buyer shipping from Bacton-Shell (OFGEM 2004e: para 1.45, p.14), suggesting the possibility that its prime concern might have been to maximise the price of its own production, the problem was, in fact, with a perfectly reasonable contractual arrangement. As we saw in the previous chapter, the degree of seasonal 'swing' (as a percentage of the average Daily Contract Quantity – DCQ) in a buyer-nominated contract is generally specified in advance and applies for a year. Seemingly whether or not the normal pricing of the contract is linked to gas or a basket of commodities including oil, should a buyer wish to nominate beyond the specified degree of swing on the upside this would be at the seller's discretion and at a premium – possibly as much as 30 percent (OFGEM 2004e: para 1.27, p.9). This both creates a disincentive for the buyer (Is the resulting price above market? It will be if the contract is market-related) and for the seller (Should the excess gas be sold now or for a potentially higher price later?) The result was that gas that was physically available for delivery was not delivered.[4]

---

4   OFGEM did in fact proceed to further investigation into the operation of Sean gas field contracts between Shell, ExxonMobil and BP (the producers) and Centrica (the contracted buyer) and concluded in June 2005 that no corporate misbehaviour occurred which resulted in gas supplies being withheld from the market (OFGEM 2005a).

The Interconnector

Further investigation of the apparent perverse behaviour of Interconnector flows also revealed no wrongdoing, but it did reveal further
detail about the complexity of factors which come into play in the
formation of UK gas prices (OFGEM 2004e: Appendix 2). Firstly,
the fact that the Interconnector continued in export mode during
October and November was not unusual – it has been the norm for
the Interconnector to be in export mode between August and October/
November.[5] Moreover, this has also been despite an NBP/Zeebrugge
price differential in favour of UK imports – although not as marked
as the one which occurred in October/November 2003. The reason
for this has simply been that shippers have been under contract to
European suppliers during this period as they build up their stocks for
the winter – and these contracts contain sharp penalties for delivery
failure, reinforced by high Belgian Cash-out penalties for imbalances.
It therefore seems that in this case too, contracts frustrated the smooth
working of the market seen purely in its short-term dimension. The only
exacerbating factor affecting 2003 was that following the usual planned
maintenance shutdown in early to mid-September, the Interconnector
suffered water ingress which reduced potential flows quite dramatically
in late September/early October (OFGEM 2004e: Figure A2.6, p.30).
The latter put shippers behind schedule and increased the risk of
incurring penalties for non-delivery.

If these were the factors coming into play from the UK side (which
meant that gas continued to leave the country), OFGEM also discovered
a complex series of factors at work on the continent which both reduced
the availability of supplies that might have been dispatched to the UK
(or substituted for the gas which shippers were obliged to deliver to
their European customers) and affected prices at the Zeebrugge hub
(such that the price differential with NBP was not as great as it might
have been). Amongst these figured a lack of supplies and liquidity at the
Zeebrugge hub caused by the non-availability of transport capacity (it is
controlled by just two companies), the relatively long duration of trades
there (Within-week or month, rather than Within-day or Day-ahead)
and the higher demand for gas in Belgium, France and the Netherlands
than had been the case in October 2002. As well as being related to
the weather, the latter was also due to factors as various as the previous
dry summer (which placed increased loads on CCGTs substituting for
hydroelectricity) and difficulties with barge shipments of coal up the

---

5   The DTI data in Figure 1.8 suggest mainly rather than wholly in export
    mode.

Rhine. In other words, it is entirely misconceived to expect that gas should automatically flow into the UK just because a short-term price signal indicates that it ought to do so – continental Europe also has to cope with unanticipated events and also has different ways of doing so. With respect to the latter OFGEM did identify one continental European supplier which had been unable to respond to UK price signals because it was bound to fulfil a Public Service Obligation (OFGEM 2004e: para 2.31, p.34), but did not discover any country-level legal obligations requiring specific storage levels to be attained at particular times of the year (OFGEM 2004e: 46–7).

August–September 2004

The most interesting aspect of the August–September price escalations is that they were quite dissimilar to their predecessors in 2003. OFGEM focused its enquiry on three possible explanations:

- demand, including the impact of Interconnector exports
- the availability of beach supplies
- the impact of increases in oil prices

Demand seemed at first as if it might have played some role – August temperatures had been 2.4 percent lower than in 2003. However, the incorporation of Interconnector flows meant that the demand on the system was actually lower than in the previous year. With respect to beach supplies problems were again identified but their configuration was quite different from that which had occurred in October and November of 2003. First of all, the reductions in terminal flows were, with one exception, at different terminals than in the previous year. They were at St Fergus-Total Oil Marine, Theddlethorpe-Conoco, Bacton-Seal, St Fergus-Mobil, Teesside-BP Amoco and Barrow. In other words only Teesside-BP Amoco figured in both price escalations. Secondly, OFGEM's investigation of the problems at these terminals reveals that they could mainly be ascribed to planned rather than unplanned maintenance (e.g. on the Frigg transportation and processing system; on the Lincolnshire Offshore Gas Gathering System and on the South Morecambe field – with the latter lasting for 40 days and reducing South Morecambe flows to zero). Moreover, only in the case of reduced flows at the Theddlethorpe-Conoco terminal were the reductions tentatively ascribed to the secular decline in UKCS production (OFGEM 2004e: Appendix 4, p.70).

This larger than normal programme of planned outages, occurring during the summer months, then came together with the impact which rapidly rising oil prices were having on continental gas prices: the upward pressure on UK gas prices normally exercised by continental prices during autumn and winter months when the Interconnector is in import mode was pulled forward a couple of months by the outages. However, and as may be observed from the Day-ahead Zeebrugge/NBP spread in Figure 4.13, the Zeebrugge positive differential was smaller during the summer months than it had been the previous year, while the autumn switchover to relatively higher NBP prices was also less pronounced than in previous years. This seeming paradox is simply explained by the fact that oil prices were pulling both indices upwards at a similar rate. It also captures quite neatly an essential difference between the character of the price shock in 2004 compared with that which occurred in 2003.

Price Relationships

Moving towards the typologies which will complete this chapter, we need to start by conducting an investigation of the relationships between various price series, first of all exclusively within the gas market and then between the gas market and other energy markets.

Within-day: OCM and OTC

The two main Within-day price series are the fully-transparent, exchange-based OCM prices and the Heren Energy Within-day Index. Using 1220 daily observations between April 6, 2000 and February 4, 2005 – observations which match the OCM SAP series with the Heren Within-day index by cutting out the weekends and bank holidays in the former series (the OCM trades continuously, whereas the Heren Index is assembled only on working days) – these two series are found to be very highly correlated (a correlation coefficient of 0.93). Moreover, the degree of correlation has been increasing over time: in 2000 (April to December) it was 0.71, in 2001 it was 0.80 but then in the last three calendar years it has been 0.98, 0.99 and 0.94. This is an interesting finding because it indicates that market participants have been acquiring the information and expertise required to move the two markets together – assisted by the fact that many if not all of the traders operate in both markets.

This in turn raises the question about whether it is in fact possible to discover which market is driving which. Because the OCM is transparent and the OTC is not, it is tempting to suggest that it is the OCM which provides Within-day price discovery for the OTC. And indeed, with the Heren Within-day Index as the dependent variable and the SAP as the independent variable, linear regression analysis does suggest that this is the case – using the above 1220 observations delivers an R-squared of 0.85. Unlagged movements in the SAP therefore seem capable of explaining 85 percent of the movements in the OTC Within-day Index.[6] However, coming to this conclusion would fail to take into account the fact that the same, relatively small group of players are trading on both the OCM and the OTC – such that causality in the opposite direction, which also produces an R-squared of 0.85, is equally possible. The traders involved may be using pricing from their OTC trades to inform their OCM offers and bids – or vice versa.

Day-ahead: Heren and Spectron

Figure 4.19 provides a snapshot of the relationship between Spectron, screen-traded Day-ahead prices and the Heren Day-ahead Index between November 2004 and February 2005. It reveals a less close relationship than that observed between the SAP and Heren Within-day

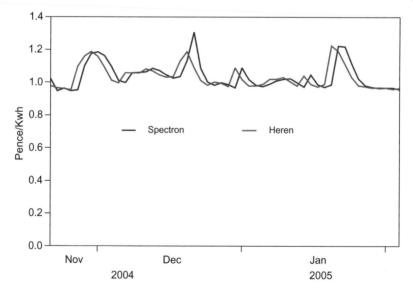

Figure 4.19: Day-ahead Prices: Heren and Spectron 22/11/04 to 4/2/05

Sources: Deloitte (2005), Heren Energy (2005)

---

6   Being Within-day series, a lagged daily relationship between them is not conceivable.

prices, but it is still positively correlated to the extent of producing a correlation coefficient of 0.63.

Month-ahead: Heren, Spectron and the IPE

Figure 4.20 shows the relationships between the Heren, Spectron and the IPE Month-ahead Indices between January 2001 and February 2005.

Despite the differences in methodology/sources of data used for the three series, the synchronisation between the series is almost perfect, indicating either perfect arbitrage or that one of the indices is the marker for the other two. The obvious candidate for the latter is the transparent, liquid and less volatile IPE Index.

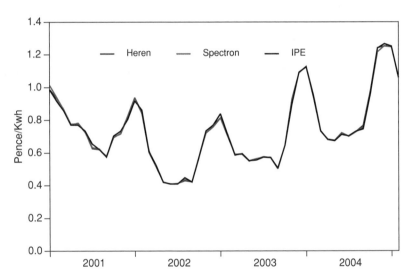

Figure 4.20: Month-ahead Indices: Heren, Spectron and IPE Compared January 2001 to February 2005

Notes: Both the Heren and Spectron Indices are volume-weighted averages of daily trades in the month preceding the delivery month (which is the index month). In the case of the Heren Index the prices involved are those reported to Heren. In the case of Spectron the prices involved are those of all trades executed through Spectron (either by phone or internet). The IPE Index is the 'final index': the unweighted average of all daily settlement prices from the expiring front month calculated on the last but one business day of that month. The daily settlement prices are the volume weighted prices of trades executed in the last 15 minutes of the IPE's business day. All three indices are for delivery to NBP.

Sources: Heren (2005); IPE (2005); Deloitte (2005)

Oil and Gas Prices

Definitely the most difficult relationship to assess is that between oil and gas prices. This is essentially because at times gas-on-gas competition appears to render the gas price autonomous of oil, while at others the oil price link is inexorably reasserted. With respect to the UK, a quite limited literature is summarised by Panagiotidis and Rutledge (2004) as generating two axioms which might explain this paradox. Firstly, from Barton and Vermeire (1999), the idea that gas-on-gas competition has weakened the link with oil prices – that gas prices can range over the wide territory between the marginal cost of producing gas and an upper limit established by the price at which gas would be substituted by oil. Secondly, from an ILEX study, the contention is that the opening of the Interconnector reintroduced a direct link with oil prices because it exposed the UK to the oil-indexed gas prices which are prevalent in continental Europe (ILEX 2001). This idea was reiterated around the same time by the legal manager of InterconnectorUK (Mulcare 2001). However, Panagiotidis and Rutledge themselves test the relationship between the price of UK gas and the price of oil between 1996 and 2003 and found both that they are cointegrated (move together over the longer term) and that this co-integration predates the opening of the Interconnector – thereby apparently contradicting the ILEX/ InterconnectorUK view that it was the opening of the Interconnector which established the oil price link. This analysis is based on the relationships between the Brent crude spot price and, respectively, the Heren Monthly Index, the SAP and the IPE front month prices – although the conclusions appear to rest more on the Brent/Heren monthly relationship than on the others.

These results give rise to a question: on what grounds should we expect a relationship between Brent spot and these gas prices – what possible causal mechanisms might be at work? With respect to the SAP, an answer is not immediately evident and we shall leave it aside for the moment. With respect to the forward and futures prices, there is a plausible argument along the lines that a particular change in spot oil prices today may well affect expectations about what the gas price should be next month. However, would such a relationship not be more strongly expressed between the IPE front month Brent price and the IPE front month gas price – with near-term expectations about oil prices influencing near-term expectations about gas prices? And might such a relationship exist in the immediate short term rather than in the long-term trends captured by co-integration? Figure 4.21 shows that such an apparently more plausible relationship does not exist, at least

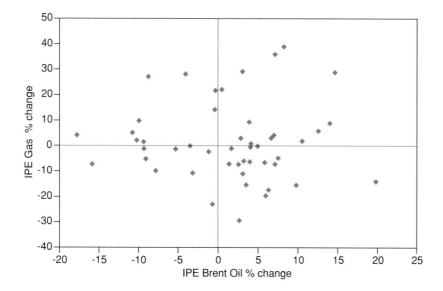

Figure 4.21: Scatter Diagram of the Percentage Changes in Front Month IPE Oil and Gas Prices between January 2000 and January 2005

Note: The Brent series underlying these changes was made compatible with the IPE front month index by averaging prices in a manner as close to the IPE Index methodology as possible: by ignoring the difference between oil and gas contract expiry dates and taking the mean of the daily Brent prices in the preceding calendar month.

Source: IPE (2005)

between January 2001 and February 2005 – the R-squared comes out around zero.

Another possibility is that gas prices are more likely to be linked with oil product prices and in particular with those of gas's nearest substitute, gasoil. Figure 4.22 explores this possibility using actual monthly gasoil prices and IPE front month gas prices between January 2000 and January 2005. Once again it can be observed, and also revealed by statistical tests, that there is no relationship between the two series.

Having reached such an inconclusive point by way of an abstract consideration of the relationship between oil and gas prices, the alternative is to begin by asking by what mechanisms UK gas prices might be linked to the price of oil and then to re-address prices with these specific mechanisms in mind. This is exactly the approach of OFGEM in its probe into the wholesale price spikes of October/November 2003 and August/September 2004 which, as we have seen, excluded a major

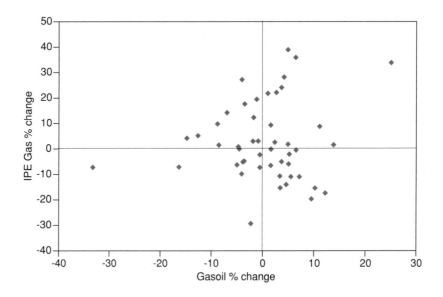

Figure 4.22: Scatter Diagram of the Percentage Changes in Gasoil Prices and Front Month Gas Prices

Notes: a) gasoil prices exclude all taxes (VAT and Duty) b) the front month gas price index is lagged by one month in order to correlate the series on an unlagged basis (e.g. February gasoil prices with the March IPE index, the latter being the average of February futures prices for March).

Sources: DTI (2005c); IPE (2005)

role for oil prices in the former, but did incorporate them into an explanation for the latter. OFGEM identifies the possible causal links between oil prices and gas prices as:

- legacy oil-indexed contracts covering a dwindling amount of UKCS gas
- the influence of oil-indexed continental gas prices exercised via the Interconnector
- the relationship between associated gas and oil production

The last of these it is supposed will serve to send gas prices in the opposite direction to oil prices – as high oil prices stimulate oil production the increasing volumes of Associated Gas will depress the gas price. However, this hypothesis is not verified empirically and is unlikely to be as clear-cut as OFGEM suggests.[7]

---

7   Eight of the top ten associated UKCS gasfields are in fact condensate fields

This means that the focus is effectively on oil-indexed gas prices which, in the case of continental gas, will exercise a 'summer effect' and a 'winter effect'. In the summer there will be a pull effect as surplus UKCS gas meets export demand from the continent – pulling up the cost of UK gas being put into storage for the winter. In the winter, on the other hand, there will be a push effect as imports of gas via the Interconnector push the oil effect into the UK.

To test the hypothesis that rising oil prices have been affecting UK gas prices via oil-indexed contracts, OFGEM postulates that there will be a lag between the rise in oil prices and any manifestation in higher gas prices. This is because of the way in which long-term indexed contracts are organised – incorporating the oil price changes of three to six months ago into the current delivery prices (OFGEM 2004a: 47). While using a lag only proves partially successful in validating the hypothesis with respect to the gas price increases of October/November 2003, it is much more successful as a partial explanation of the behaviour of forward prices over the winter of 2004–05. This success is based on relating Q4 2004 and Q1 2005 forward gas prices to three-month lagged front month Brent (OFGEM 2004e: Figure A5.4, p.87). A coefficient relating oil to gas of 1.2 is subsequently arrived at for the 'winter effect', although it is also acknowledged that this estimate may be conservative given that an alternative estimate from the *Utility Journal* is as much as 1.6 (OFGEM 2004e: 91). Note that in both cases the impact on gas prices is more than proportionate.

Gas and Other Energy Prices

In investigating the causes of the gas price increases in October/November 2003, OFGEM did consider the possibility that gas prices could have been moved by either coal or electricity prices. However, the conclusion was negative because although coal prices were also escalating this had not led to any substitution of gas for coal in electricity generation (OFGEM 2004a: 50). Likewise with electricity: although the 'spark-spread' (the differential between electricity input and output prices) had increased during October 2003, this implied increase in

---

for which a normal expectation that gas production would increase pro-rata with liquids production may be disturbed by reinjection to recover more of the more valuable liquids. Moreover, the other two top ten fields are oil fields in their declining 'blow-out' phase – oil production is declining and they are being turned into gasfields. For example, since 1992 the Brent field has been undergoing the world's largest depressurisation project to recover an additional 1.5Tscf of gas and 34MMstb of oil (Kuyper 2002).

the profitability of gas-fired generation did not lead to any increased contribution from gas-fired generators. Rather, the increase in the spark spread allowed gas-fired generators to maintain their output despite increasing gas prices (OFGEM 2004a: 53).

Wholesale Gas Price Formation

In now seeking to develop the foregoing discussion into typologies of wholesale price formation in the UK, we can conceptualise different processes as involving interactive combinations of supply-side triggers, demand-side triggers, timing and response conditioners. These are:

> **Supply-side Triggers**
> Planned Maintenance
> Unplanned Maintenance
> Secular Decline in UKCS Production
>
> **Demand-side Triggers**
> High Level of Seasonal Demand
> Unanticipated Fluctuations in Daily Demand
>
> **Timing**
> Summer
> Autumn
> Winter
> Spring
>
> **Response Conditioners**
> Interconnector response
> Stock response
> Contractual friction
> OCM profiling

Figure 4.23 then assembles the particular clusters of these factors which have been linked with the price increases of October/November 2003 and August/September 2004. As may be observed, the genealogy of each event is quite different. They are particularly distinguished by the need to run-down (interrupted rebuild) stocks during the first, October/November 2003 event (Figure 4.24), while in August/September 2004 the Interconnector delivered the shortfall by way of lower export flows and, on a couple of days in September, significant imports. Both responses, however, served to raise prices, the latter combining both summer pull and winter push effects to bring high oil-related prices into the UK.

	October / November 2003	August / September 2004	Hypothetical
	Autumn	Summer	Winter
Field Decline	Yes	Yes	Yes
Planned Maintenance	Yes	Yes	No
Unplanned Maintenance	Yes	Little	Yes
Interconnector Response	Export	Import	Import
Stock Response	Interrupted Rebuild	None	Run-down
Contract Friction	Yes	No	Yes
OCM Profiling	No	No	Yes
Unanticipated Daily Demand	No	No	Yes
High Seasonal Demand	No	No	Yes
Low Seasonal Demand	No	No	No

Figure 4.23: Price Formation Typologies

To these typologies we add a hypothetical one which includes three other factors that might conceivably be involved in price formation: daily and seasonal influences on the demand side and the destabilising impact of OCM profiling which we have linked with unplanned upstream maintenance. It should be noted that low seasonal demand in the form of a warm winter can be just as destabilising as a cold winter – giving rise to significant collapses in first quarter prices as holders of storage are caught in long positions and engage in rapid stock run-downs (Figure 4.24 – see also Farrington 2004). Also, it should be borne in mind that unplanned maintenance may not just affect producing gas fields – between 1999 and 2004 force majeure was declared three times at the Rough storage field (Farrington 2004). As we have seen (Figure 4.14), on January 29, 2004 this brought about a very dramatic surge in the SAP.

Operationalising these effects more precisely, with respect to the October/November event, OFGEM did try out some estimates of the price elasticity of supply in order to assess whether the observed changes in prices might have some predictability in relation to the reductions in available volumes represented by unplanned and planned maintenance, increased Interconnector exports to catch up with shortfalls caused by

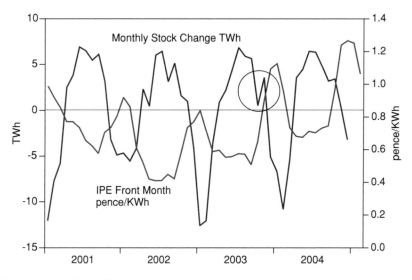

Figure 4.24: Stock Changes and Prices

Sources: IPE (2005); DTI (2005b)

maintenance and increased Interconnector exports to meet increased continental demand. Using all these factors simultaneously indicated an implied price of 45–49 pence per therm (OFGEM 2004e: Table A3.5, p.60) – well above the highest actual out-turn of 34 pence per therm.

A similar ex-post exercise is also conducted with respect to the forward prices over the winter of 2004–05 – attempting to assess whether the observed increases in forward prices were reasonable in relation to expectations about costs. This is particularly important for two reasons: first of all because the main impact of the kind of extreme price event which has been under the spotlight tends to be on forward/futures prices and, secondly, as we have previously pointed out, the effective price of gas today is a weighted average of forward/futures prices from the past. The exercise is initially (using a mild winter weather scenario) able to explain 11 pence per therm or 54 percent of the observed 20 pence per therm increase in the forward price. Of this 11 pence, 6 pence or 35 percent was the summer and winter effect (3 pence each) of continental oil prices, 2.5 pence due to the increased likelihood of a demand-side response (interruptions), 1.5 pence due to the increased likelihood of peak-shaving gas being required and 1 pence due to increased storage costs (OFGEM 2004e: 96). The only way in which the methodology could deliver a price estimate close to the actual outcome was under the assumption that market participants were expecting a 1 in 50 winter.

This margin of uncertainty leaves some loose ends, which are reflected in the increasing volatility of forward and futures prices, from day ahead to month out. On the one hand, there is a relatively small group of traders which seems to have become increasingly proficient at dealing with Within-day trading and with synchronising the different marketplaces. On the other hand, moving forward, the number of traders and liquidity decreases, while risks may assume an increasing variety of permutations. Unplanned maintenance can strike at any part of the UKCS infrastructure, and at any time, while large programmes of unsynchronised planned maintenance taking place during the summer can exercise a decisive impact on winter stocking, both in the UK and on the continent. There is also the Interconnector paradox: if it fails to respond to UK price signals, UK prices rise; if it does respond, they still rise if the oil price is putting upward pressure on continental gas prices. Finally, the links between oil and gas prices are still far from being tied down. OFGEM, as we have seen, has investigated links which have a 'physical' manifestation in the way oil-indexed contracts are drawn up. But this cannot be exhaustive: can it really be the case that if there were no oil-indexed gas contracts in Europe, there would be no link between oil and gas prices? And how can the co-integration between spot oil and spot (SAP) gas prices found by Panagiotidis and Rutledge be explained from within the oil-indexed contract paradigm? The latter is a relationship that we left aside earlier in the chapter, but which now leads us to consider another possibility − that gas traders who are also upstream producers directly link both their wholesale market and futures/forward trades with the oil price or, alternatively, use their trading power in a way which achieves the same effect. Given the increasing prevalence of NBP price-related long-term contracts, there could also be an incentive to do so.

CHAPTER 5

REGULATED COSTS: TRANSMISSION AND DISTRIBUTION

Introduction

Given the political spotlight which has been on wholesale prices, and the attention which we have just been giving them, it is perhaps easy to overlook the fact that gas costs only constitute a part, and for many final consumers a minority part of the price of gas which they pay. On the way to final consumers there are two other costs which, depending upon which group of final consumers we are addressing, may well constitute the majority of the price of gas. These two costs are, firstly, transmission and distribution costs, and, secondly, supply costs.

Here, in this chapter, we address transmission and distribution costs – which are quite distinct from other costs in the gas chain because they are *regulated*. At this point along the road towards the final consumer therefore regulation enters the process of gas price formation. While the task of charting the path of these regulated costs will present us with some empirical challenges later in the chapter, for the moment the required exposition is quite straightforward. First of all, we shall introduce the main physical characteristics of the UK's gas transmission and distribution system, something which was left until now rather than being included in the introductory chapter. Secondly, we shall describe and analyse the history of the regulation of these 'monopoly core' network costs. Finally, we look at the impact of this regulation on the behaviour of these network costs, unravelling their differential impact on different classes of consumer and exposing their role in price formation.

The UK's Transmission and Distribution System

The general characteristics of the UK's national gas transmission system (NTS) and local distribution zones (LDZs), are shown in Figure 5.1. Some of them we have already encountered in other contexts, but detail on the physical characteristics of the system is new and requires further elaboration.

Market Opening	Since 1998 all gas consumers can choose their Supplier
Regulator	Office of Gas & Electricity Markets (OFGEM)
Third Party Access	Regulated
Type of tariff	Shipper pays NTS Entry, NTS Exit, LDZ and Customer charges
No. of Transporters	Transco plus 14 other small transporters
No . of Shippers	154, but some owned by same parent company Some shippers are also suppliers
No. of Suppliers	43 supplying both domestic and non-domestic markets 67 supplying non-domestic market only. Some suppliers owned by same parent company Some suppliers are also shippers
No. of Storage Operators	5 storage facility operators including Transco LNG
Pipeline length	Transco system has 275,000 Kms of mains pipeline of which 6,400 Kms are the National Transmission System
System Entry Points	21 Aggregate System Entry Points of which 6 Beach Terminals
System Exit Points	12 Local Distribution Zones containing 33 Exit Zones from National Transmission System, plus 49 directly supplied large industrial sites and 2 Interconnectors
Customers	Around 21 million individual customers

Figure 5.1: The General Characteristics of the UK's National Gas Transmission and Local Distribution Systems prior to new entry in Distribution

First of all the distinction between the national and local systems is one of pressure (and therefore capacity). The 6,400 kms of NTS is high pressure (up to 85 bar) and is shown in Figure 5.2. Gas enters the NTS through *Connected Delivery Facilities* which include:

i)   Facilities for processing gas produced from offshore or onshore oil or gas fields
ii) Facilities for the storage of gas
iii) Pipeline systems operated by other public gas transporters
iv) Pipeline interconnectors by which gas is transported from another country
v)   Any other pipeline or pipeline system

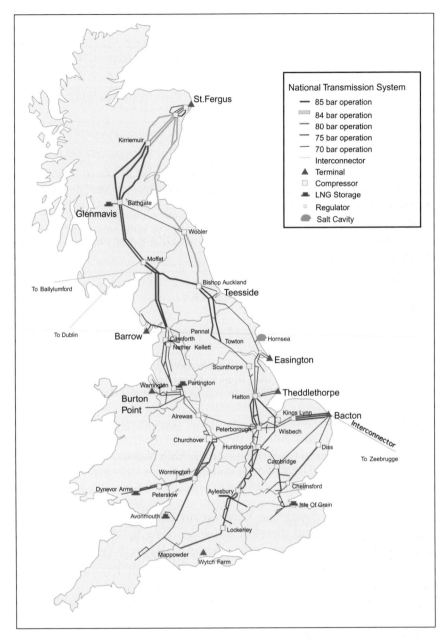

Figure 5.2: UK National Transmission System

Source: National Grid Transco (2005)

The gross calorific value of gas entering the system varies between 37.5 MJ/m³ and 43.0 MJ/m³ measured at standard conditions of temperature (15°C) and pressure (1013.25 mbar). Determination of the precise CV of gas in the system is carried out according to international standards and is measured at the beach terminals and other locations on the Transco system, in total about 110 locations.

Twenty-four compressor stations then drive the gas through the system to 140 offtake points (*NTS Exit Points*) from where it is delivered to 40 power stations, a small number of major industrial customers and the 12 *Local Distribution Zones*. These contain the *Local Transmission System* with pipelines operating at pressures up to 38 bar, and the *Distribution System* in three pressure tiers: 2−7 bar, 75 mbar−2 bar and below 75 mbar.

For management purposes the twelve LDZs are grouped into eight *Distribution Networks* as follows:

Scotland
North of England (North + Yorkshire)
North West
East of England (East Midlands + East Anglia)
West Midlands
Wales and the West (Wales + South West England)
South of England (South + South East)
London

To determine how much gas has been transported for each shipper ideally every input and output should be metered each day. However, with around 18 million individual supply points, this is uneconomic so Transco must estimate this based on actual historical data. The starting point is to divide the country into zones for which the total output demand can be measured each day – these are the LDZs and are based on groups of offtakes from the NTS. Then the measured quantity for each LDZ is divided up between the shippers who supply gas to that LDZ. Larger sites within the LDZs which are directly metered are measured and then subtracted from the total LDZ output. The residual quantity is then allocated to the shippers supplying non-daily metered sites, according to an agreed formula. At a later date, there is a reconciliation between initial estimates of demand and the historical actual demand calculated via a sampling process.

On a particular day, a customer's supply point may receive its gas via any of the offtakes within its LDZ. However, on the day of highest (peak) demand there is an optimum arrangement in which the offtakes serving each supply point can be precisely identified. The points for

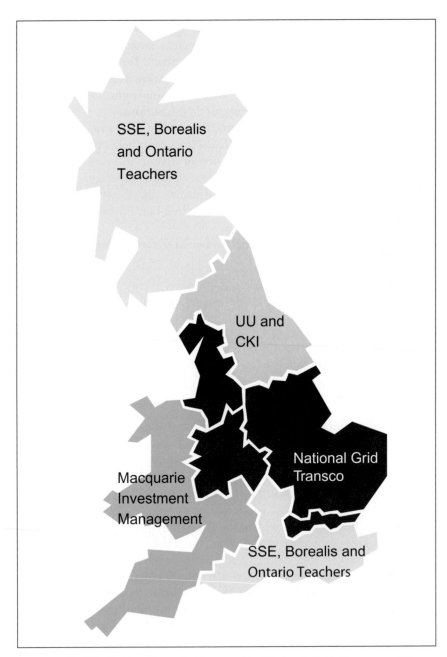

Figure 5.3: Distribution Networks Operated by National Grid Transco and New
Entrants

Source: National Grid Transco (2005)

each offtake on a peak day are therefore grouped into another type of zone (an 'Exit Zone') of which there are 33 and which are identified by their area code numbers (see Table 5.3 below). An 'individual system point' is a single pipeline through which gas flows into or out of the system. A 'system point' is an 'individual system point' or a group of such points which may be either NTS system points or LDZ system points. Classes of system points include

(i)   'Individual System Entry Points', 'System Entry Points' and 'Aggregate System Entry Points'
(ii) 'Individual System Exit Points' and 'System Exit Points'.
(iii) NTS/LDZ Offtakes
(Network Code, A-1.4.2, A-2)

Aggregate System Entry Points

The most important entry points are groups of two or more known as 'Aggregate System Entry Points' (ASEPs), of which there are currently 21, including the six large beach terminals:

(i)   Bacton (Norfolk)
(ii)   Barrow (Cumbria)
(iii) Easington (Humberside) + the Rough storage facility
(iv)   St Fergus (Grampian Region)
(v)   Teesside (Cleveland)
(vi)   Theddlethorpe (Lincoln)

plus the proposed new LNG terminals at Milford Haven. All 21 ASEPs are listed in Table 5.1, along with their 'Baseline Entry Capacities'.

Exit Points

Gas is taken off the NTS via 'System Exit Points' of which there are three main classes:

(i)   'NTS Supply Points' consist of points at which gas is conveyed directly from the NTS to particular consuming premises and which are 'Supply Meter Points'. NTS Supply Points must have an annual consumption greater than 58,600,000 KWhs/yr (2,000,000 Therms/yr.)
(ii) 'Connected System Exit Points' which comprise one or more individual exit points which are not supply meter points. These include connections to a pipeline system operated by a Gas Transporter other than Transco, Storage Facilities and Interconnectors.

(iii) 'NTS/LDZ Offtakes' are the NTS Exit Points comprising all the individual system points at which gas flows out of the NTS into a particular LDZ.

Supply meter points are either *daily metered* or *non-daily metered*, with the former either firm or interruptible. Those supply meter points on the NTS are all daily-metered. As we have seen, some LDZ exit points are daily-metered – they meet the minimum consumption level of 58.6 million KWh – the rest are non-daily metered.[1]

The Regulation of Transmission and Distribution

While Figure 5.1 describes the current status of third party access to the UK's Gas Transmission and Distribution network as being 'regulated', this was not initially the case. Moreover, how the 'monopoly core' of the network was to be regulated has evolved over time – as apparently simple prescriptions turned out to be not so simple in practice.

Third Party Access

Third party access to the transmission and distribution network is the enabling cornerstone of competition: without it competition between suppliers for final consumers could not have developed. The right of access by independent shippers (third party suppliers or their transportation agents) to the British Gas pipeline system actually preceded privatisation, having been provided for by the *Oil and Gas Enterprise Act 1982*. But this Act proved to be without issue, particularly because it had offered no specific guidance on the method of charging for transportation services. The Gas Act of 1986 (which privatised British Gas) subsequently provided some small advances: although it was thought unnecessary to lay any new general duties on British Gas to facilitate common carriage, Section 19 of the 1986 Act provided for a company which wished to use the British Gas pipeline system in order to deliver its own gas to its own customer, to apply to the Director General of OFGAS for 'directions' which would secure the right of 'common carriage' through the British Gas pipeline.[2] Initially access was therefore

---

1   The registered user of a supply point whose annual consumption exceeds 73,200 KWh/yr (2,500 Therms/yr) may request to become a Daily Metered Supply Point (Network Code G - 1.5.9).

2   'Common Carriage' is a specific form of third party access under which pipeline capacity is allocated between shippers on a pro-rata basis – in contrast to the

negotiated rather than *regulated* – suppliers had to negotiate access prices with British Gas – while price control regulation was applied only at the level of the totality of British Gas' activities, supply together with transmission and distribution.

However, the difficulty of achieving *non-discriminatory access* to the network under this kind of arrangement quickly became apparent as, between privatisation in 1986 and 1990, no third parties had materialised amid claims of price discrimination and difficulties in negotiating access with British Gas. The solution though, which involved three referrals to the Monopolies & Mergers Commission in 1988, 1993 and 1997 and a review by the Office of Fair Trading in 1991, went way beyond simply establishing the principle of non-discrimination. Actually putting this principle into practice led inexorably to the unbundling of transportation from supply in order to make the costs of transportation separately transparent, something which, as we saw already in Chapter 3, in turn gave rise to the requirement for a Network Code which would govern the behaviour of the newly unbundled actors: transporters, shippers and suppliers. And none of this would amount to anything without competitors having access to a bigger share of the market, such that there would be an increasing demand for third party access. This involved both access to customers and access to gas.

Third party access therefore only became *regulated third party access* once five sets of changes had been made over almost a decade between 1988 and 1997:

- making upstream gas available to British Gas' competitors (begun following the 1988 Monopolies & Mergers Commission report and consolidated in 1992 by way of British Gas releasing gas from its upstream contracts);
- increasing the number of customers available to British Gas' competitors by reducing the eligibility threshold to 2,500 therms per year (1992), and ultimately by opening the domestic market to competition (started in 1996 and completed in 1998);
- unbundling transportation from supply (this happened internally within British Gas in 1994 as Transco came into being and was followed in 1997 by separation of supply and transportation into separate businesses, Centrica and BG plc);
- placing a separate regulatory price control on transportation (the first control ran from 1994 to 1997);
- establishing standard rules and procedures for third party access, including those which were required for the residual gas balancing

---

alternative of allocation on a first-come-first-served basis.

of the system (the first version of the Network Code was introduced in 1996).

Regulatory Pressure and Fragmentation

Once these conditions for regulated third party access had been firmly established, after 1997 the emphasis shifted to making regulation more effective – essentially in order to achieve a reduction in the costs of transmission and distribution. This effort had two major components. On the one hand, the price control regime was made tougher and more complex. On the other hand, the process of pricing access was addressed by way of the 1999 New Gas Trading Arrangements which also, as we have seen, marketised gas balancing by introducing the OCM. With respect to access pricing the New Gas Trading Arrangements inaugurated auctions – it being perceived that this was the way to introduce competition into the pricing process. In this section we shall only address the changes in the price control regime, leaving access pricing to be addressed separately as an integral part of using the system (next section).

Transco's 1997–2002 Price Control was the outcome of what may be described as the 'mother of all regulatory battles'. The review had started with a consultation in June 1995 and only ended with OFGAS' final proposals in February 1998, with the Monopolies & Mergers Commission enquiry of 1997 in between. The context was Transco's high profits, underspend on capital expenditure, concern about quality of service and public discontent about 'fat cat' salaries.[3] The resulting price control was unprecedented, involving not only RPI-5 percent, but also a draconian base year price cut of 21 percent. However, the 1997 Price Control is not just of interest because of the severity of the control, but also because of regulatory innovation. The price cap was split 50/50 between a fixed revenue cap and a volume driver and was further structured to distinguish between large and other users. The latter change was introduced because larger loads directly connected to the NTS imposed lower incremental costs on Transco.

The 2002 Price Control then added significantly to the complexity of the regulatory regime by opting for 'asset-specific' regulation which fragmented the regulatory regime to reflect Transco's different functions as:

---

3   At the time, the author in tandem with Ian Rutledge showed TransCo to be the most profitable among an international selection of gas transportation companies – work which was published in the 1997 Monopolies & Mergers Commission report (Rutledge & Wright 1997).

- National Transportation Asset Owner (TO)
- Local Distribution Zone (LDZ) owner and operator
- National Transportation System Operator (SO)
- provider of metering services and meter reading services

Transco's NTS (TO) and LDZ operations continued to be regulated under an RPI-X formula (with the former representing 16 percent of revenues and the latter 70 percent), but they did face a slightly different base-year price reduction (OFGEM 2001b). Moreover, because there were growing doubts about the impact of cost-reducing regulation upon capital investment, an additional system of 'output incentives' was grafted onto the existing form of regulation. These took the form of allowing Transco to earn a rate of return higher than 6.25 percent (its existing regulatory rate) when making new investment in pipeline capacity, provided this was justified by 'market signals' emanating from auctions of long-term entry capacity (see below).

For the NTS (SO) function, the revenues for which were now to be separately derived from the commodity charge (while the TO function would derive its revenues from capacity charges – see below), an entirely different genre of incentive regulation was introduced: on the grounds that while Transco faced significant pressure to reduce internal costs, this was not the case with respect to external costs such as energy balancing and entry-capacity buy-backs. The incentives were both carrots (additional profits) and sticks (penalty payments), capped within certain limits.

For LDZs asset-specific regulation also involved the introduction of indicator-led quality of service targets (OFGEM 2001c) – in an effort to address the following concern:

> … while the RPI-X model of price control has so far been successful at delivering both improved cost efficiency and a high quality of service from Transco and other price-controlled utilities, there are concerns that in the future cost savings may be at the expense of quality of service.
>
> Source: OFGEM (2001d: 1)

Finally, and most recently, the regulation of transmission and distribution has taken another complex twist in connection with National Grid Transco's sale of four LDZ regions as described in Chapter 2. While the introduction of one of the regulatory changes implied by these sales, separated LDZ price controls in order to improve efficiency by way of 'comparator regulation', was already being considered even under Transco's unitary ownership, serious potential problems for the regional distribution of revenues had been identified (OFGEM

2002d; OFGEM 2002e). In addition to this the actual fragmentation of the distribution network has affected the whole gamut of network governance, raising a whole series of problems concerning licensing, the ability to discriminate, the interface between the NTS and distribution networks and security of supply (gas balancing). OFGEM has responded (2004f, 2004g), but it will only be possible to discern the implications for price formation once the new regime has settled down and its actual costs can be observed.

Pricing Access

In distinguishing pricing access from regulating access, we are in no way suggesting that price control regulation has no bearing on the price of access. Rather, in this section we are looking at access from the perspective of the user of the system – in terms of how the user is actually charged and how these charges have been arrived at by Transco.

In Figure 5.1 we noted that shippers pay 'NTS Entry, NTS Exit, LDZ and Customer charges'. But behind this apparently simple statement there lies an agonising past and a complex present. The agonising past involved both creating the required costing information and developing a pricing methodology. The costing information needed to be created because as a monolithic, integrated organisation British Gas had no tradition or requirement for costs to be allocated internally between different activities. Developing a pricing methodology involved, at a general level, the choice of cost of capital and how to value assets plus, more specifically, how to allocate costs to particular customer groups (especially how peak loads should be paid for) and how to determine the appropriate proportions of 'capacity' and 'commodity' charges in prices.

1988–1999

Prior to 1999 the evolution of the pricing discussion moved through three stages. At first (in 1988), British Gas said it did not use cost-based pricing at all – claiming that it could not do so because final prices were determined by the presence or absence of competitive pressure in the market place. Then (in 1993), British Gas presented a methodology to the Monopolies & Mergers Commission investigation of that year. This involved a 50:50 capacity to commodity charge split and, in calculating the capacity charge, the use of marginal cost estimates for different transmission pipeline sizes. The capacity charge was allocated to different customer classes in relation to their claims on peak capacity.

Subsequently, after internal unbundling, British Gas adopted a Long-run Marginal Cost (LRMC) approach for calculating the capacity charge for access to the National Transmission System, while proposing Average Accounting Cost for regional transmission and distribution (OFGAS advocated Average Incremental Cost). The capacity to commodity charge split was changed to 65:35. Charging based on distance was abandoned in favour of standard matched pairs of entry and exit charges derived from LRMC.

Competitive Access Pricing

Under the original Network Code arrangements introduced in 1996, Transco was able to sell unlimited amounts of entry capacity at the main terminals at fixed prices. Similarly there were no disincentives for shippers to limit the amounts of capacity they bought. When severe capacity constraints occurred at the St Fergus terminal in 1998, Transco had to buy back entry capacity at what were considered to be excessively high prices; these costs were ultimately passed on to consumers. To remedy this problem, auctions of Monthly System Entry Capacity (MSEC) for tranches of up to six months were introduced as part of the New Gas Trading arrangements in September 1999, with auctions to be held twice yearly. This was intended as a non-discriminatory method of rationing the provision of entry capacity rights. Shippers could also trade capacity with one another. Auctions of Monthly Interruptible System Entry Capacity (MISEC) followed in December 2000.

Deeming the auctions to MSEC to have been a success, OFGEM subsequently concluded that auctions could also be used as a tool for determining the long-term investment requirements of the system. In January 2003 Long-term System Entry Capacity (LTSEC) auctions were introduced for sales of entry capacity at the 19 Aggregate System Entry Points (the coastal terminals, storage facilities and interconnectors), in quarterly strips, for the years out to 2017 (52 quarterly periods from Q4 2004 to Q3 2017). Subsequently the periodisation was changed to be aligned with Transco's price control formula year (April–March) with the second round held in August[4] 2003 for the period beginning two years (approximately) ahead (April 2006) with the final quarter starting 1 January 17 years ahead (2019). The amount of LTSEC on offer in each auction was 80 percent of a baseline quantity determined

---

4   Because of August holidays the auctions are now held in September.

by Transco's price control, with the remaining 20 percent available for auctions of MSEC and daily capacity.

Shippers who flow more gas through an entry point than they have purchased in the auctions face overrun charges intended to act as a strong incentive for them to purchase sufficient quantities of entry capacity (for example they may be charged for any overrun at eight times the highest price in any auctions of firm capacity).

The LTSEC auction methodology is based on a system whereby amounts of baseline plus potential incremental entry capacity investment at a particular Aggregated System Entry Point (ASEP) are offered at reserve prices in ascending order (step prices) such that if the whole of an incremental tranche of capacity were sold at the relevant reserve (or step) price, the revenue received by Transco would cover the cost of providing that increment (i.e. the long-run marginal cost). The LTSEC auction is conducted over ten days at the end of which Transco allocates amounts of entry capacity to successful bidders at notional clearing prices and decides whether the level of demand exhibited in the auction justifies the provision of any incremental capacity which may be either permanent (obligated) or temporary (non-obligated). A rather complicated set of rules determine whether Transco should actually build permanent incremental capacity. These are published in Transco's Incremental Capacity Release Statement. To date, the LTSEC auctions have indicated high demand for entry capacity in early years at St Fergus but only low demand at other ASEPs and generally declining volumes in later years at all existing ASEPs, which may reflect expectations of increasing North Sea gas field depletion.

Following the annual LTSEC auction, Monthly System Entry Capacity (MSEC) and any unsold LTSEC are offered for two years ahead in auctions held in February each year. Subsequently, any unsold MSEC is sold each month in a Rolling Monthly System Entry Capacity (RMSEC) auction. Finally any unsold LTSEC, MSEC and RMSEC are released via Daily System Entry Capacity (DSEC) auctions and Daily Interruptible System Entry Capacity (DISEC) auctions on either a Day-ahead or Within-day basis.

The way in which the LTSEC auctions work may be further examined and understood with the help of Tables 5.1 and 5.2 and Figure 5.4. Table 5.1 lists the Aggregate System Entry Points (ASEPs) together with their 2003–04 capacity and the 'baseline' capacities assumed for the 2003 and 2004 auctions.

Table 5.2 then provides a numerical working through of the process whereby prices are raised in steps to bring capacity into line with demand. At the baseline capacity of 1342 GWh/day it can be seen that

Table 5.1: Aggregate System Entry Points and Capacity

Aggregate System Entry Point (ASEP)	Type	Baseline Capacity GWh/day 2003/4	Baseline Capacity GWh/day, for Sept.2003 Auctions	Baseline Capacity GWh/day, for Sept.2004 Auctions
Bacton	Coastal Terminal	1646	1481	1655
Barrow	Coastal Terminal	790	711	711
St Fergus	Coastal Terminal	1721	1549	1628
Teesside	Coastal Terminal	823	741	751
Theddlethorpe	Coastal Terminal	628	565	791
Milford Haven	Coastal Terminal	0	0	0
Easington/ Rough Storage	Coastal Terminal/ Storage	985	887	1027
Hatfield Moor (onshore field)	Onshore Field and Connections	1	1	1
Wytch Farm	Onshore Field and Connections	4	3	3
Burton Point	Onshore Field and Connections	61	55	55
Hole House Farm	Onshore Field and Connections	29	26	26
Garton	Storage Site	0	0	420
Hatfield Moor (storage)	Storage Site	60	54	54
Hornsea	Storage Site	195	176	175
Glenmavis	Storage Site	110	99	99
Partington	Storage Site	239	215	215
Aldborough	Storage Site	259	233	n.a.
Barton Stacey	Storage Site	0	0	0
Cheshire	Storage Site	0	0	214
Avonmouth	Constrained LNG Storage	165	149	149
Dynevor Arms	Constrained LNG Storage	55	50	50
Isle of Grain	Constrained LNG Storage	243	219	218

Sources: Transco PGTL (Special Condition 28B, Schedule A); Transco (2003; 2004)

Table 5.2: Long-term Capacity Auctions: Supply, Demand and Step Prices

Capacity Potentially Available (GWh/day)	Price Step	Price (pence/peakdayKWh/day)	Expression of Future Demand (GWh/day)
1510	P5	0.0229	1223
1476	P4	0.0222	1286
1443	P3	0.0214*	1386
1409	P2	0.0212	1471
1376	P1	0.0204	1498
1342	P0	0.0198	1596

*   notional clearing price

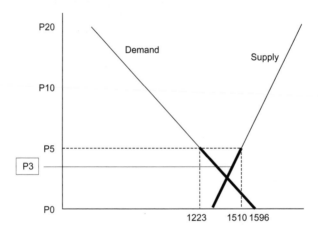

Figure 5.4: A Representation of Long-term Auctions

demand at 1596 is way above the capacity being made available, but as the price is increased in steps, the capacity that could be made available increases and demand decreases until they are approximately brought into line at price step 3 (0.0214 pence/KW). At this point capacity demanded is equal to or less than, but not greater than, the capacity on offer. Figure 5.4 expresses this iteration graphically. Whether this pricing process is appropriately conceptualised as an 'auction' is doubtful given that it is the seller rather than the buyer who bids the prices. Moreover, this process is further managed by the rule that shippers have to bid in reducing volumes as the price steps increase – so that the demand curve cannot be other than downward sloping.

Returning to the charges for the current use of the system, short-term capacity auctions are in fact only responsible for the determination of one of the six charges which go to make up the price of access. As Figure 5.5 shows, as well as National Transmission System Entry Capacity charges, there are NTS Exit Capacity charges and NTS Commodity charges plus Local Distribution Zone Capacity and Commodity charges plus Customer charges. The NTS 'Commodity' charge is fixed, while LDZ Capacity and Customer charges are fixed according to Supply Point Offtake Quantity (SOQ) and LDZ. Commodity charges are fixed according to both SOQ and the quantities being shipped. This leaves NTS Exit charges which vary according to location and are listed in Table 5.3.

Duration of use	Shippers may book system capacity on a quarterly, monthly, daily firm or daily interruptible basis.
	Auctions for Quarterly Capacity held annually for capacity years +2 to +16
	Auctions for Monthly Capacity held annually for capacity years +1 and +2
Periodisation	The 'Capacity Year' lasts from 1st April to 31st March
Tariffs	For NTS Entry 'Capacity', determined by auction with reserve prices,
	NTS Exit 'Capacity' fixed according to location of NTS Exit Zone or Direct Supply Point.
	NTS 'Commodity' Charge at 0.0177 p/KWh transported.
	LDZ 'Capacity' fixed according to Supply Point Offtake Quantity (SOQ)
	LDZ 'Commodity' Charge fixed according to size of load and Supply Point Offtake Quantity (SOQ)
	'Customer' Charge fixed according to Supply Point Offtake Quantity (SOQ)
Indicative Total Tariff	Charge for transportation to large customer: 0.230 p/KWh
	Charge for transportation to small customer: 0.482 p/KWh
Interruptible capacity	Transportation to a designated interruptible supply point is charged neither NTS Exit Charges nor part of the LDZ charge. There is a credit paid by Transco to the Shipper for interruption in excess of 15 days in a capacity year.
Secondary Market	Entry capacity can be traded between shippers on OTC market

Figure 5.5: Types of System Use, Duration and Tariffs 2004

Table 5.3: NTS Exit Capacity Charges for LDZ Zones 2004

Distribution Network	*LDZ Exit Zone*	*Pence per Peak day KWh per day*
East of England	EA1	0.0026
	EA2	0.0095
	EA3	0.0034
	EA4	0.0102
	EM1	0.0028
	EM2	0.0006
	EM3	0.0073
	EM4	0.0059
North of England	NE1	0.0001
	NE2	0.0019
	NE3	0.0008
	NO1	0.0001
	NO2	0.0007
London	NT1	0.0193
	NT2	0.0125
	NT3	0.0139
North West	NW1	0.0078
	NW2	0.0069
Scotland	SC1	0.0001
	SC2	0.0009
	SC4	0.0001
South of England	SE1	0.0102
	SE2	0.0193
	SO1	0.0134
	SO2	0.0183
Wales and The West	SW1	0.0075
	SW2	0.0143
	SW3	0.0283
	WA1	0.0100
	WA2	0.0172
West Midlands	WM1	0.0061
	WM2	0.0066
	WM3	0.0073

Source: Transco (2004)

The Cost of Access

We are now in a position to address the cost of access – in order to be able to relate the cost of transmission and distribution to price formation. This we shall do in two different ways. First of all, we shall conduct our own estimate of transportation costs for both large and small loads, at the same time demonstrating how the different charges discussed above contribute to the final overall transportation cost. These estimates will then be compared both with transportation cost data provided to us by Transco and with the final price of gas paid by different classes of customer – the latter to establish the proportion of final price which is represented by transportation costs. We shall also look at the trends in the overall cost of transportation.

Costing Loads

Table 5.4 provides an illustration of how the transportation cost for a large load would be calculated, while Table 5.5 does the same for a small customer. The main point to note about both of these estimates is that NTS Entry Charges make up either a small or a very small minority of the transportation cost: about a quarter in the case of the large load and less than 2 percent in the case of the small load. In other words a great deal of regulatory time and company expense has

Table 5.4: Calculation of Unit Transportation Charge for Shipment to a Large Customer

Type of Charge	*Calculation*	*Total Charge*
NTS Entry Capacity	$365 \times 100{,}000$ KWh $\times 0.0324$p	£11,826
NTS Exit Capacity	$365 \times 100{,}000$ KWh $\times 0.0193$p	£7,044.50
NTS Commodity	$20{,}000{,}000$ KWh $\times 0.0177$p	£3,540
LDZ Capacity	$(0.2115\text{p} \times 100{,}000 \text{ KWh}^{-0.1806}) \times$ $100{,}000$ KWh $\times 365$	£9,636
LDZ Commodity	$(0.7369\text{p} \times 100{,}000 \text{ KWh}^{-0.2121}) \times$ $20{,}000{,}000$ KWh	£12,821
Customer (Capacity)	$(0.0366\text{p} \times 100{,}000 \text{ KWh}^{-0.2100}) \times$ $100{,}000$ KWh $\times 365$	£1,204.50
TOTAL		**£46,072**
Charge per KWh shipped	£ 46,072 / 20,000,000 KWh	0.230 pence

Assumptions
Shipper has a *Daily Metered* customer in London (Exit Zone NT1) with an annual consumption of 20 million KWh per year and a registered *Supply Point Offtake Quantity* (SOQ) of 100,000 KWh/day. Entry Point is St Fergus where capacity has been booked in the January 2003 Quarterly Entry Capacity Auction at the step price of 0.0324 pence per KWh/day.

Table 5.5: Calculation of Unit Transportation Charge for Shipment to a Small Customer

Type of Charge	Calculation	Total Charge
NTS Entry Capacity	365 x 151.4 KWh x 0.0024p	£ 1.33
NTS Exit Capacity	365 x 151.4 KWh x 0.0193p	£ 10.67
NTS Commodity	20,000 KWh x 0.0177p	£ 3.54
LDZ Capacity	365 x 151.4 KWh x 0.0481p	£ 26.50
LDZ Commodity	20,000 x 0.1284p	£ 25.68
Customer (Commodity)	20,000 x 0.1430p	£ 28.60
TOTAL		**£ 96.33**
Charge per KWh shipped	£96.33 / 20,000 KWh	0.482 pence

Assumptions
Shipper has a *Non-daily Metered* customer in London (Exit Zone NT1) with an annual consumption of 20,000 KWh. This would place the customer in Category E0301B (< 73,200 KWh/year) with an assumed load factor of 36.2 percent. Thus the customer's SOQ would be 20,000 ÷ (365 x 0.362) = 151.4 KWh. Entry Point at Barrow where capacity has been booked in the January 2003 Quarterly Entry Capacity Auctions the baseline reserve price of 0.0024 pence per KWh/day.

been put into designing auctions for a minor part of the overall cost of transportation. It is the LDZ charges which make up the largest part of costs, not NTS Entry Charges: in these estimates 51 percent of the transportation costs incurred for the large load are LDZ charges, rising to 84 percent for the small load.

Transportation Cost and Final Prices

Table 5.6 first of all demonstrates that our own illustrative calculations of transportation costs approximate very reasonably to Transco's own for December 2003. Secondly, it provides some idea – and it is important to stress 'some' because of the methodological problems discussed in the notes – of the relative importance of transportation costs for different classes of consumer. This very broadly shows that for domestic consumers transportation cost represented around 30 percent of final price, for firm manufacturing loads between 20 and 30 percent, for interruptible manufacturing loads between 10 and 20 percent and for power station loads less than 10 percent.

A different approach to measuring the proportion of final prices which is represented by transportation costs is to consider data generated

Table 5.6: Transco Cost Estimates and Cost as Proportion of Final Price

Consumption Category	Type of consumer	Annual Consumption (KWh) Dec. 2003	Transportation Price			Final Price	Proportion of Final Price
			NTS p/KWh	LDZ p/KWh	Total p/KWh	p/KWh	%
0-73,200 KWh		8,500	0.0608	0.4245	0.4853		
		19,000	0.0607	0.4237	0.4844	1.62→1.82	29.9→26.6
	average domestic	20,500 KWh					
Own Calculation Table 5.5	**20,000 KWh**	**20,000**			**0.4820**		
		30,000	0.0606	0.4236	0.4842		
73,200-732,000		150,000	0.0625	0.3087	0.3712		
		600,000	0.0625	0.2809	0.3434	1.2980	26.5
> 732,000 (Firm)	non-domestic commercial and industrial	1,500,000	0.0599	0.2327	0.2926	1.0950	26.7
		6,000,000	0.0581	0.1724	0.2305	1.0950	21.1
Own Calculation Table 5.4		**20,000,000**			**0.2300**		
		30,000,000	0.0536	0.1167	0.1703	0.8750	19.5
		150,000,000	0.0500	0.0797	0.1297	0.8750	14.8
						0.8750	
> 732,000 (Interruptible)		15,000,000	0.0362	0.0752	0.1114	0.8750	12.7
		30,000,000	0.0362	0.0657	0.1019	0.8750	11.6
		150,000,000	0.0362	0.0482	0.0844	0.8750	9.6
NTS (Firm)	**Power Stations**	6,000,000,000	0.0430	-	0.0430	0.740	5.8
NTS (Interruptible)		6,000,000,000	0.0362	-	0.0362	0.740	4.9

Table 5.6: continued

Notes: Transco's transportation cost estimates are national averages as at December 2003, while our own calculations with which they are compared are more specific (see Tables 5.4 and 5.5). In estimating the proportion of final price represented by transportation costs, a number of problems had to be confronted. First of all, average UK domestic gas prices are only available on an annual basis, the 2003 data in fact refer to the period Q4 2002 to Q3 2003, they include VAT, they are only available for individual categories of consumer (credit, direct debit and pre-payment) and they are calculated assuming an average consumption level of 18,000 KWh per annum (DTI 2005c: Table 2.3.3). Above we therefore **(a)** accept that there is no alternative to using the UK domestic gas price averages (unit values) for 2003 **(b)** adopt the closest transportation price band to the consumption level assumed for calculating this average gas price (19,000 KWh per annum) **(c)** indicate the range of average domestic prices (the direct debit average price constitutes the lower end of the range, the pre-payment price the upper). Secondly, with respect to non-domestic prices, the only available series is based on surveys of manufacturing industry only (DTI 2005c: Table 3.1.2) and these are in size categories (small=less than 1.5million KWh; medium = 1.5million to 8.8million KWh; large=greater than 8.8 million KWh) which are not a particularly good match for the transportation cost categories. They are however available on a quarterly basis. We have therefore opted only to use the average final gas prices paid by small and medium-scale manufacturing consumers, linking these up illustratively with transportation costs as follows: small consumers' Q4 2003 average price with the 600,000 KWh transportation cost estimate; medium consumers' Q4 2003 average price with both the 1.5million KWh and the 6million KWh transportation cost bands. Thirdly, there is only one interruptible gas price series available − a quarterly average for the manufacturing sector as a whole (DTI 2005c: Table 3.1.2). This is therefore illustratively linked with all the interruptible non-power sector transportation loads/cost categories, using the Q4 2003 price. Finally, there is only one price series available for power station gas supplies − a quarterly average (DTI 2005c: Table 3.2.1). This is therefore illustratively linked with both the firm and the interruptible power station load transportation cost estimates, again using the Q4 2003 price.

Sources: National Grid Transco (2005); own calculations (Tables 5.4 and 5.5); DTI (2005c)

---

on the buy side of the market − making use of the transportation cost data provided by British Gas (Centrica). These data are aggregated for two main customer groups: all business customers and all residential customers. For calendar year 2004 it shows that transportation cost represented 23.3 percent of turnover for British Gas' business customers and 30.1 percent for residential customers (Centrica 2004: 9 and 11). This appears to be entirely consistent with our sell-side calculations.

These proportions will of course vary over time as final prices, supply costs and wholesale gas prices change. In 1995, for example, OFGAS estimated that transportation charges made up 44 percent of an average domestic bill and between 25 percent and 34 percent of the final price for firm industrial loads (OFGAS 1996: Vol 1, p.9). The changes for British Gas customers between 2001 and 2004 are in Table 5.7 and show that the 2004 proportions were probably the lowest on record.

Table 5.7: Estimated Transportation Charges for British Gas Customers 2001–2004

Year	BUSINESS (Centrica Business Services)		RESIDENTIAL (British Gas Residential)	
	pence/ KWh	*Transport Cost as % Turnover*	*pence/ KWh*	*Transport Cost as % Turnover*
2001	0.294	28.3	0.579	37.4
2002	0.343	27.6	0.548	33.0
2003	0.384	28.6	0.576	34.9
2004	0.331	23.3	0.572	30.1

Notes: The pence/KWh estimate is arrived at by dividing the segment transportation cost (transmission, distribution and metering) by an imputed volume (Centrica does not directly provide segment volume data in its Annual Report, but confirmed that the imputation methodology used generates the actual volume). Both the Centrica Business Services and British Gas Residential business segments of Centrica plc trade under the British Gas name.

Source: Centrica (2004, 2003, 2002)

In addition to these changes in the relative importance of transportation charges, changes in their absolute values may be observed in both Table 5.7 and in Figure 5.6. Figure 5.6 shows Transco's nominal (money of the day) unit revenue declining consistently and considerably between 1995 and 2000, before picking up a little over the last three financial years. Despite the latter, real unit revenue in 2003–04 was clearly very substantially below the 1995 figure. While British Gas' pence/KWh data in Table 5.7 cannot be expected to exactly mirror the upward trend in Transco's nominal unit revenues after 2000 because specific factors come into play (larger average loads reduced British Gas' Business transportation costs in 2004, while Residential benefited from an NTS credit in 2002), its behaviour is not inconsistent with the Transco data.

From this information about the behaviour of transportation costs over time and about their relative importance for different customer groups, we can draw three important conclusions to both end this chapter and establish links with the next. Firstly, because of the different relative importance of transportation costs for different categories of

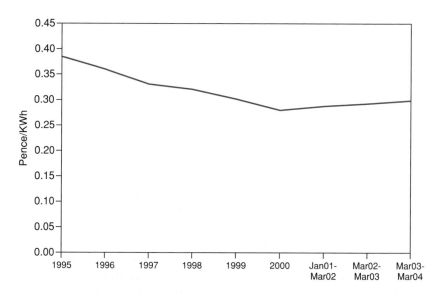

Figure 5.6: Transco's Average Revenue per KWh Transported 1995–2004

Notes: The Transco revenue figure used for this calculation is the Transco revenue data for third party sales, including metering and meter reading (the latter were unbundled from transportation in April 2000). Pre-1997 data are as restated (from a current cost to a modified historical cost basis) in the 1997 *Annual Report & Accounts* of BG plc. Post 2000 Transco's Regulatory Accounts are used and the changeover from a calendar year to a March financial year is handled as it is in those accounts. The volume data are 'Gas input to Transmission System' from the Department of Trade and Industry, using monthly data to exactly match the periodisations used.

Sources: BG plc (1997), Transco (various years), DTI (2004b)

customer, primarily according to size of load and secondarily according to interruptibility, movements in wholesale gas prices should have a differential impact: most on NTS firm and interruptible customers and least on domestic customers. Secondly, the regulation-induced decline in nominal transportation unit revenues, particularly during the 1997 to 2002 regulatory period, means that all categories of consumer were being rendered more vulnerable to movements in wholesale prices. Thirdly, any increase in final prices experienced during 2003 and 2004 can certainly not be either wholly or partly ascribed to the behaviour of transportation costs. In particular, the relative stability of transportation unit costs for British Gas' residential customers in 2004, coupled with a sharp decline in the proportion of turnover which they represented is ample indication of both a rise in final prices and one that transportation costs did not contribute to.

CHAPTER 6

FINAL GAS PRICES

Introduction

As we arrive at the end of the gas chain, at the 'burner tip', we encounter so-called 'final prices' and thereby data which are at least misty and sometimes rather foggy. First of all, final prices should not be confused with 'retail prices' – the latter are a sub-set of final prices, but do not delineate the entire territory. Also included are prices to non-domestic customers (industrial, commercial and government consumers) who are not normally considered to be retail customers because they pay negotiated rather than posted (advertised) prices. Moreover, these customers are sometimes referred to as 'wholesale customers', which they may be if they are purchasing gas directly from wholesale markets. Otherwise, they are better described as 'contract customers', leaving the word wholesale attached exclusively to what we have previously, in Chapter 4, analysed as wholesale markets. We will thus encounter non-domestic prices, which will generally be commercially confidential contract prices, and domestic prices, which are posted retail prices.

Secondly, liberalisation has cast a veil over the data, making it a job of work to find out what is happening to final prices. Previously, a single monopoly supplier fixed domestic prices for everyone and a limited range of tariffs for non-domestic customers. Now, competition has generated a plethora of prices which vary according to which supplier is chosen. In addition, non-domestic prices remain confidential, while different forms of payment (credit, direct-debit and prepayment) and devices like dual fuel deals and add-ons can make domestic retail prices opaque. Thirdly, and as we have already noted, the markets linked with the final consumption of gas generate relatively little data compared with the daily flood from wholesale markets.

Non-Domestic Prices

These problems leave us with the following raw material to work with. For the contract market there are only indicative data in the form of three price series, two covering the manufacturing sector and one for power generators' gas input prices. These are all published by the UK government Department of Trade & Industry and are based on surveys which it conducts. The first and principal series, covering manufacturing industry, has the following characteristics:

- It is available on a quarterly basis, covers Britain only (England, Wales and Scotland), is exclusive of tax (VAT) and has versions including and excluding the Climate Change Levy (which was introduced in April 2001).
- Since 1988 it has been based on a survey of 1,200 manufacturing sites (now referred to as the 'Quarterly Fuels Enquiry'), distinguishing between small, medium and large customers and also providing data for the median and the 10 percent and 90 percent deciles.
- In 1990 two further sub-series were introduced covering Firm and Interruptible prices.

The second series also only covers gas prices to manufacturing industry, although it is often confusingly described as covering 'industrial' gas prices (and therefore ought to include non-manufacturing industries, such as construction, but apparently does not). It has the following characteristics:

- It is available on a quarterly basis, stretches back to 1970, but is only published as an index: the Department of Trade & Industry does not release the raw price data behind the index.
- Like the first series it is based on a survey, but this time of *gas suppliers* and not customers. Moreover, the survey is not restricted to Britain: it covers the whole of the UK.
- The series is not disaggregated in any way, except to include or exclude the Climate Change Levy.

The third series, covering the price of gas paid by power generators, commenced in 1993 – once the construction of gas-fired power stations, which had been non-existent before 1990, had got under way. The series is published by the UK Department of Trade & Industry and is based on a quarterly enquiry of electricity generators. 'The prices reported are typically for long-term contracts, with price escalator factors, some of which may have been entered into some time ago. As such the prices can be higher than those paid by large industrial users who typically negotiate prices each year' (DTI 2005c: A27, p.88).

Domestic Prices

Here there are two principal sources of data, both generated by the Department of Trade and Industry. The first is the gas price component of the UK Retail Price Index (RPI). This is gathered along with the other price data which go to make up the RPI from monitoring gas prices at a large number of locations throughout the country. In the second quarter of 1994 VAT was levied on gas sales for the first time at a rate of 8 percent, a rate which was subsequently reduced to 5 percent in the fourth quarter of 1997. Post 1994, therefore, the RPI gas price component includes these indirect taxes. A historical series net of VAT has however been constructed, both in nominal and real terms.

The second source is derived from a quarterly survey of all gas suppliers in the UK household market. This survey includes all prices available to household customers which, combined with an average consumption level deemed to be 18,000 KWh, are used to generate three representative bills (small, average and large) for each of the 12 LDZs and for each payment category (credit, direct debit and pre-payment). These bills are in turn divided by the average consumption level to derive an average unit cost, by area, payment category and also in aggregate for the whole of the UK. These implied average prices all include VAT.

This survey also provides the raw material for estimating prices by scale of consumption: in providing data to Eurostat this is done for six customer categories, while the DTI itself publishes for three size categories for the purposes of an international comparison.

'Beach' Prices

The last series of prices which we need to introduce because it plays an important role in the ensuing analysis is not in fact a final price – it is the so-called 'beach price'. This series is simply the unit value derived from the volume and total value of gas sales into the UK, the data for which are gathered as part of the Department of Trade & Industry's quarterly enquiry into oil and gas extraction. It isolates sales into the UK market by taking UKCS production and sales plus net imports. It therefore provides an indicator of average market prices received by upstream gas producers for initial (or 'beach') sales into the UK.

Overview and Analytical Approach

In order to place recent developments in UK final gas prices in context, Figure 6.1 shows the trends in the prices of gas to both industry and households on a quarterly basis since 1986.

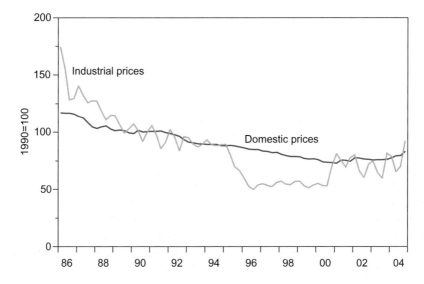

Figure 6.1: Indices of Real Gas Prices to Industry and Households 1986–2004

Note: while the DTI designates one of these series as 'industrial', it apparently only covers representative prices to manufacturing industry (as discussed above in the text). Both series exclude VAT.

Source: DTI (2005c)

They show a gentle, secular decline in the price of gas to households between 1986 and the end of 2000, followed by a gradually increasing trend. The behaviour of gas prices to industrial consumers has been quite different: unlike prices to households they were punctuated by a substantial slump in the mid-nineties for which a combination of UKCS overproduction and competition in the contract market was responsible (Rutledge and Wright 2003). Thereafter, from mid-2000, these prices have been both moving upwards and displaying more pronounced seasonal variations than had been the case in the past. Indeed, there is a sharp contrast between the relative stability and unresponsiveness of prices to households and the behaviour of prices to industry.

Analytical Approach

In considering final gas price formation in this chapter, we are essentially trying to weigh three possible influences over changes in final prices: changes in the cost of gas itself, changes in the cost of the transportation element in final price and changes in the supply mark-up (supply costs and profits). And these three influences must be considered separately in relation to both domestic and industrial consumers. As a secondary issue we shall also be considering price differentials within each of these two segments of the market.

In weighing the importance of the three possible influences over final prices, we already anticipate that changes in transportation costs will not have had any major influence over price formation. This is because the evidence in Chapter 5 revealed that transportation costs have been relatively stable since 2000 (Figure 5.6). The corresponding implication is that the cost of gas and the supply mark-up are the key variables. We shall therefore first of all examine the statistical relationship between gas cost and the final price of gas, in the case of the domestic market referring to work carried out by OFGEM as part of its *Domestic Competitive Market Review*. Secondly, we shall infer what has been happening to supply margins by bringing together the data on the changing cost composition of final prices.

Final Price Formation in the Non-domestic Market

Gas Costs, Prices and Supply Mark-ups

Figure 6.2 provides data for both parts of the analysis of the non-domestic market. First of all it plots the dependent variable, the most representative final price, which we have selected as the average quarterly price of firm gas to manufacturers. Secondly, it plots two potential independent (causal) gas cost variables: the 'beach price' (shaded in blue) – a rough proxy for the purchase of gas under long-term beach contracts at average prices – and the IPE front month index (shaded in red). The latter is selected because, as we saw in Chapter 3, it is probable that part or all of the gas costs paid by suppliers for their gas will be priced using a link to short-term markets, and the IPE's front month index is the most popular in this respect.

These series emerge first of all as relatively highly correlated (coefficients of 0.79 and 0.77 for the manufacturing average and beach prices and the IPE Index respectively) and then as exhibiting a relatively strong causal link from gas costs to final prices (R-squares around 0.6), with the link between beach prices and average prices for firm delivery to manufacturing industry being slightly stronger than that between the IPE index and these final prices.

The changes in the cost composition of final prices, also shown or implied by Figure 6.2, now allow us to indicate what has been

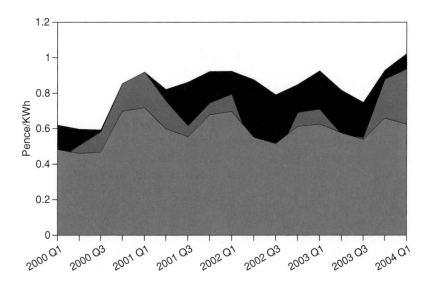

Figure 6.2: Gas Costs and the Average Price of Gas for Firm Delivery to Manufacturers

Note: This Figure is 'unstacked', such that each series is superimposed on the previous one(s). The blue-shaded area plots the movements in beach prices, the red-shaded area plots the movement in a quarterly average of the IPE front month index and the black-shaded area plots the movements in average prices for firm delivery.

Sources: DTI (2005c); IPE (2005)

happening to supply mark-ups (to cover supply costs and profits), and thereby also one of the main reasons why final non-domestic prices are not wholly responsive to changes in wholesale prices. The differences between the final price series and each of the two gas cost series are shown in Table 6.1 and indicate the possible sizes of the margin available to cover both transportation costs and the supply mark-up. In the case of the difference between the average price of gas for firm delivery to manufacturing industry and the beach price, it is always positive but probably only sufficient to cover the likely transportation costs for a firm manufacturing load (see Tables 5.4 and 5.6 and Figure 5.6 in Chapter 5) – and in some quarters probably not even that. Secondly, because the IPE front month index shows a substantial premium over the beach price (indicated by the area shaded in red), wholesale gas bought at this price would reduce still further the margin available to cover transportation costs and the supply mark-up – indeed for two

quarters this comes out as negative. Even taking into account the fact
that the IPE front month index is for delivery to NBP, and therefore
includes the entry charge portion of transportation costs, makes no
material difference – entry capacity charges will at most contribute
only a quarter of transportation costs for industrial consumers (see
Table 5.4 in Chapter 5).

Table 6.1: Margins over Beach and Futures Prices at the Average Final Price to
Manufacturers (pence/KWh)

	Firm Price minus Beach	Firm Price minus IPE One Month Index
2000 Q1	0.138	0.195
2000 Q2	0.136	0.090
2000 Q3	0.125	0.011
2000 Q4	0.117	-0.039
2001 Q1	0.191	-0.009
2001 Q2	0.224	0.064
2001 Q3	0.308	0.245
2001 Q4	0.243	0.176
2002 Q1	0.226	0.128
2002 Q2	0.325	0.426
2002 Q3	0.275	0.365
2002 Q4	0.237	0.157
2003 Q1	0.300	0.215
2003 Q2	0.241	0.248
2003 Q3	0.209	0.199
2003 Q4	0.269	0.051
2004 Q1	0.398	0.087

While these data can only aspire to provide some indication of the
factors shaping final gas price formation for final non-domestic consumers, it does allow three general conclusions. Firstly, and as one might
anticipate, final prices in the non-domestic market are largely driven
by movements in wholesale prices. Secondly, to the extent that they
are not, this is due to variations in the supply mark-up: to competition
forcing suppliers to absorb part of any increase in wholesale prices.
Thirdly, if gas cost has been tied to the IPE front month index, then
the position looks worse – liberalisation has incurred costs, equal to
the red-shaded area in Figure 6.2. This has been the price of moving
away from long-term contracts, the cost of the new risks, and it seems
to have made it difficult for suppliers to secure adequate and stable
margins. Only the largest non-domestic consumers seem to offer suppliers a prospect of consistent profitability – underwritten by lower
gas costs than average and much lower transportation costs – a point

which the withdrawal of BP from the small-scale industrial market appears to substantiate.

However, there may be a further twist here: it may not in fact be the case that margins have been squeezed pro-rata with increases in gas costs which are linked to futures prices. This is because profits are made by traders and brokers within the red-shaded area of Figure 6.2, and many traders are suppliers. In turn we are therefore left with a hypothesis – that suppliers can make money in the non-domestic market to the extent that they are successful traders.

Differentials

Differentials in the non-domestic market are illustrated by the differentials established by the Quarterly Fuels Enquiry which, as we have noted, only covers the gas prices paid by manufacturing industry. These

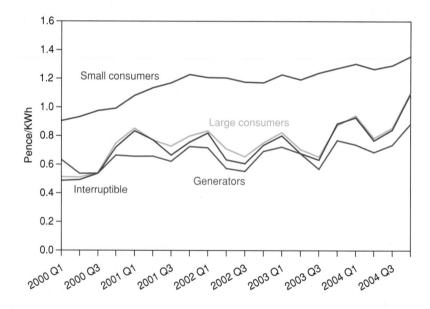

Figure 6.3: Price Differentials in the Non-domestic Market

Note: the Quarterly Fuels Enquiry designates an annual consumption level greater than 8.8 million KWh as 'Large' and less than 1.5 million as 'Small'. Respondents purchasing more than one type of supply (tariff, firm or interruptible contracts) are treated as separate entities in respect of each type of supply (DTI 2005c: Table A3, p.88)

Source: DTI (2005c)

show, first of all, that the prices paid by large consumers and those manufacturers taking interruptible supplies are virtually identical and move together in a seasonal pattern. Secondly, these prices are closely tracked at a slightly lower level by the prices which generators pay for their gas. However, the seasonal pattern of the prices paid by generators does appear to be a little smoother, perhaps reflecting the effect of different (e.g. longer-term) contracting arrangements.

Thirdly, there is a very large differential between the prices paid by the largest consumers and those paid by small consumers and this cannot be wholly explained by the differential transportation cost for these classes of consumer. Until the fourth quarter of 2004, the differential varied between about 0.36 pence per KWh and as high as 0.58 pence per KWh, substantially more than the differential transportation cost indicated by the calculations in Tables 5.4 and 5.5 in Chapter 5 (0.25 pence per KWh). The lack of pronounced seasonal fluctuations in the prices paid by small manufacturing consumers also makes the behaviour of these prices appear more like those of captive retail customers – and indeed, a relatively larger volume of tariff custom can be expected in this size category.

Final Price Formation in the Domestic Market

Figure 6.4 provides some historical background to the analysis in this section by plotting the difference between changes in retail gas prices and changes in the retail price index since the year before privatisation in 1986. Until April 2002, when both gas and electricity retail prices were fully liberalised, the behaviour of domestic gas prices reflected the changes in the regulatory regime detailed in Figure 6.5: the regime was of the 'RPI minus X' variety such that gas price increases were, to various extents, less than the rate of inflation (and therefore shown in black in Figure 6.4). After April 2002, and to a small extent beforehand with only capped differentials in force between April 2001 and April 2002, the unfettered operation of the market has clearly produced a much less favourable outcome for consumers. But the question is to what extent has this been justified by, for example, escalating gas costs? To help answer this question while also exploring price formation for domestic customers we can turn to OFGEM's 2004 *Domestic Competitive Market Review*, one of the concerns of which was to establish whether 'domestic customers are benefiting from the changes in wholesale prices to the extent that would be expected in a competitive environment' (OFGEM 2004b: p.79).

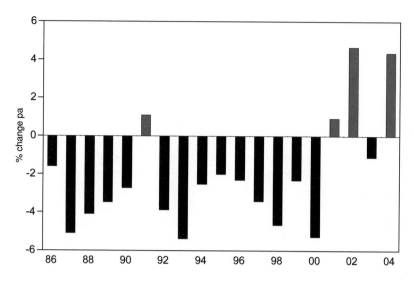

Figure 6.4: Annual Percentage Changes in Retail Gas Prices minus Annual
Percentage Changes in the Retail Price Index 1985 to 2004

Note: Retail Gas Prices are the gas component of the Retail Price Index exclusive
of VAT. The black columns denote the years when the percentage change in the
Retail Price Index was greater than the percentage change in retail gas prices; the
red columns denote the opposite.

Source: DTI (2005c)

Regulatory Period	Gas Cost	Transportation	Supply
1987–1992	Pass-through		X = minus 2
1992–1994	Capped Pass-through		X = minus 5
1994–1997	Capped Pass-through	X = minus 5	X = minus 4
1997–2002	Pass-through with economic purchasing test until 2000; Capped until April 2001	X = minus 2 (from April 1998) applied to a split (50/50) revenue cap/volume-driven cap; base-year P = minus 21; Storage unbundled under separate regime	X = minus 5 (tariff cap on British Gas only) until 2000; X = minus 4.5 (tariff cap on non-Direct Debit customers only) until April 2001; capped differentials until April 2002

Figure 6.5: Regulation of Gas Costs, Transportation and Supply 1987–2002

In the context of our approach to price formation for domestic customers, this means that OFGEM is interested in how the behaviour of just one of its three cost components may be influencing the price of gas, namely the wholesale cost of gas. Moreover, in the case of retail prices, this question is *a priori* problematic because one would not necessarily expect to find any clear relationship between movements in wholesale prices and movements in final retail prices: as we have already been able to observe, unlike non-domestic prices retail prices exhibit smooth and relatively gentle movements – in sharp contrast to the volatility of wholesale gas prices. In addition, and as OFGEM comes to reflect, there are a series of reasons why the behaviour of the actors involved would be likely to exclude any clearly articulated relationship between wholesale and retail prices. These reasons include (OFGEM 2004b: 91, *italics our own observations*)[1]:

- the fact that suppliers may price to reflect the complex contract structure of their supplies, rather than just movements in relevant forward prices: to reflect the 'Weighted Averaged Cost of Energy' (WACOE) *(something which we already anticipated at the end of Chapter 3)*;
- the fact that vertical integration may dilute retail price responsiveness because e.g. profits made upstream can compensate for a squeeze on profits downstream *(as we demonstrated would be and is a strategy in Chapter 2)*;
- the fact that suppliers may smooth prices to domestic consumers *(which they obviously do)*;
- the fact that competition with other retail suppliers may prevent price adjustments of the 'cost plus' variety.

It therefore comes as some surprise that OFGEM's regression analysis does purport to discover a 'fairly strong' relationship between wholesale gas prices and direct debit retail prices. Unpicking how OFGEM arrived at this conclusion provides an explanation. Selecting retail prices to direct debit customers as the representative final price for domestic customers, OFGEM uses a monthly series running from June 2000 to February 2004.[2] Average transportation charge costs for Britain are then stripped out of these prices in order to better capture 'the impact of wholesale prices on the competitively driven elements of the domestic price' (OFGEM 2004b: 89). The resulting series, net of transportation

---

1 OFGEM makes these points in the context of the relationship between electricity wholesale and retail prices, but they are equally valid with respect to gas.
2 The price data are OFGEM's own and are not published for general consumption.

costs, is then regressed against monthly NBP gas prices, leading to the conclusion that 'in the long run, the percentage change in retail price is 43 percent of the change in the wholesale price' (OFGEM 2004b: 90). While this is a relatively weak relationship in terms of a complete explanation for the behaviour of domestic gas prices, OFGEM claims that it is a strong demonstration that final gas prices have been responding in an appropriate manner to changes in wholesale gas prices — that reductions and increases are being passed on more or less *pro rata*. This is because OFGEM has calculated that wholesale gas prices represent about 51 percent of final prices, such that the maximum response of final domestic gas prices to changes in wholesale gas prices should be 51 percent of the latter. Unfortunately for OFGEM this overlooks the fact that in order to conduct the analysis transportation costs representing 34 percent of the final price for direct debit customers were stripped out of the final price – meaning that, for the purposes of OFGEM's regression, the wholesale gas cost represented 77 percent and not 51 percent of the gas price net of transportation costs which OFGEM was investigating. Therefore the extent to which movements in domestic gas prices reflect movements in gas costs falls well short of what OFGEM was seeking to demonstrate.

Despite these efforts by OFGEM, we are therefore left with a weak relationship between the wholesale cost of gas and the final price of gas to domestic customers even if transportation costs are excluded from the calculation. And why this should be the case becomes readily apparent once the role of the third component in final price, supply mark-up, is taken into account.

From Table 6.2 and Figure 6.6 it can first of all be seen that the supply mark-up to the domestic consumer (costs of supply plus profit margin) represents a quite substantial portion of the final price of gas such that, if we were to replicate OFGEM's methodology and strip out the transportation costs, supply costs would make up 22 percent, 36 percent, 32 percent and 33 percent of 'competitively driven elements of the domestic price' in 2001, 2002, 2003 and 2004 respectively. This would of course serve to reduce the strength of the relationship between wholesale gas prices and the final price less transportation costs.

Secondly, in 2002 the beach price cost of gas dipped (Table 6.2) but, coinciding with the full liberalisation of the domestic market, final prices actually rose – such that the supply cost margin jumped from 13 percent to 22.5 percent. Subsequently, in both 2003 and 2004, when the beach price cost rose again, final prices rose again such that the supply cost mark-up was more or less maintained. In other words, this indicates that suppliers in general have been pursuing a strategy in

Table 6.2: Cost Components of Domestic Gas Prices

	Direct Debit UK Average less VAT	*Beach Price*	*IPE Front Month*	*Transportation Cost (British Gas Residential)*	*Supply Mark-up (using Beach Price as Gas Cost)*	*Supply Mark-up*
	– – – – – – – *pence per KWh* – – – – – – –					*percent*
2001	1.41	0.647	0.760	0.576	0.18	13.0
2002	1.48	0.601	0.591	0.548	0.33	22.5
2003	1.54	0.650	0.677	0.579	0.31	20.3
2004	1.63	0.710	0.876	0.572	0.35	21.5

Notes: the Domestic price used is the average UK direct debit price, excluding VAT. Transportation Cost is British Gas' transportation cost to its residential customers (see Chapter 5). Supply mark-up is a residual which includes supply costs and profits.

Source: DTI (2005c); Centrica (2004, 2003, 2002)

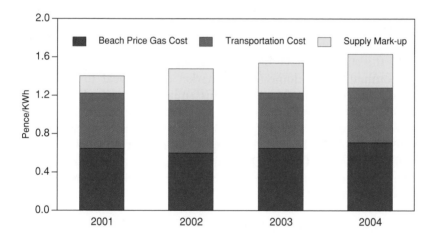

Figure 6.6: Cost Components of Domestic Gas Prices

which domestic prices have been unresponsive to gas costs when these have been moving in a downwards direction, but responsive when they have been moving upwards. It also indicates that it is the behaviour of the supply mark-up (i.e. price changes at the discretion of suppliers) rather than the wholesale cost of gas which caused domestic gas prices to run ahead of inflation in 2002. This particular conclusion is unaffected if the IPE front month index, rather than the beach price, is selected as the appropriate marker for gas costs – Table 6.2 shows that the IPE index also moved downwards in 2002. On the other hand, it could be argued that if the IPE index were to be taken as a proxy for gas costs in 2003 and 2004, then supplier price increases would emerge in a better light, particularly for 2004 when this futures price rose dramatically more sharply than the beach price (Table 6.2). Such an argument would however have to contend with three issues: that the precise extent to which the IPE index prices wholesale gas is not known; that in any event this price provides insurance against risk and as such contains a cost which is more properly a 'supply cost' than a 'gas cost' and that, despite escalating futures prices, British Gas still managed to increase its residential gas profits in 2004 – as we saw at the end of Chapter 2.

Corroboration of the current size of supply cost margins indicated by the above data comes from OFGEM itself. In the 2004 *Domestic Competitive Market Review* OFGEM conducts what it calls 'headroom analysis' – which estimates by how much a new entrant to the gas market might be able to discount prices relative to the incumbents and still earn a reasonable rate of return. OFGEM estimated that headroom in gas supply ranged from about 6 percent to about 14 percent depending on the size of customer base (OFGEM 2004b: Figure 5.1, p.137). In other words, the small number of large gas suppliers identified in Chapter 2 as dominating the domestic gas market does appear to be enjoying excess profit margins. Moreover, this situation, in which the supply mark-up is over 20 percent, may be contrasted with the situation which prevailed before the opening of the domestic market to competition: in 1995 OFGAS estimated the supply mark-up at only 10 percent of the final price (OFGAS 1996: Vol 1, p.9). That this has happened should come as no surprise given both the costs and increased risks of competitive supply.[3]

Differentials

Figures 6.7 and 6.8 show the movements in domestic gas price differentials from two perspectives – by payment category and by scale of consumption. By payment category, the substantial differential enjoyed by direct debit over credit and prepayment customers is clear. However, interestingly given that the direct debit customer is seen as the main beneficiary of gas-on-gas competition, the differential has been closing since the domestic market was completely freed of price controls in April 2002: since 2001 prices for direct debit customers have risen

---

3   The costs have been exacerbated by the excessive prices per customer paid during takeovers (see OFGEM's demonstration of this (2004b: 141) and the analysis in Rutledge & Wright (2003)).

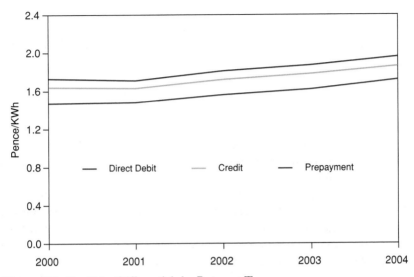

Figure 6.7: Gas Price Differentials by Payment Type

Note: Prices are UK averages including VAT

Source: DTI (2005c)

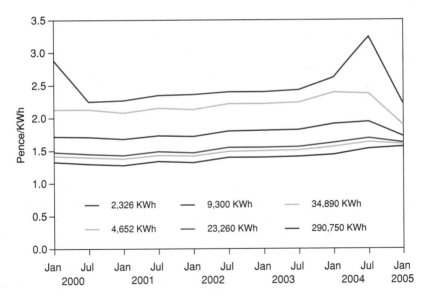

Figure 6.8: Gas Price Differentials by Scale of Consumption

Note: Prices exclude VAT

Source: Eurostat (2005)

by about 16 percent, compared with 14 percent for the other two categories.

The data on the behaviour of prices according to scale of consumption are from Eurostat, using the more detailed breakdown which this source offers compared with the DTI's *Quarterly Energy Prices* (six size categories, compared with the DTI's three).[4] Its recent behaviour appears strange: after a relatively lengthy period of stable differentials, these first widen sharply during 2004 and then close up equally sharply. While no complete explanation can be offered for this, the middle of 2004 was when British Gas (Centrica, accounting for 60 percent of the residential market) increased its prices by 12.4 percent. This change then interacted with the two-tier price band which has replaced standing charges, reinforcing the effect of the price increases in the summer months when gas consumers are consuming relatively little and a much higher proportion of their consumption is therefore priced in the first, higher priced band. In the case of British Gas this first price band applies to 12.5173KWh per day of consumption and has a tariff which is 43 percent higher than the second tier band which applies to levels of consumption beyond 12.5173KWh times the number of days in the bill period. In the winter months (e.g. January 2005 in Figure 6.8), the opposite effect comes sharply into play – there was no tariff increase at this time and high levels of winter consumption would place a much smaller proportion of consumption in the higher priced band, thereby reducing the unit cost of a bill (which is what Figure 6.8 shows) very sharply. These effects are more potent the lower the annual level of consumption.

Price Competition by Customer Category

Figure 6.9 provides an unsophisticated but effective demonstration of the degree of competition in the different customer segments of the UK's domestic gas market – and how this changed as price control regulation was completely lifted in April 2002. As part of its quarterly survey of the prices being paid by domestic customers for their gas, the Department of Trade & Industry generates not only average price estimates in each customer category (e.g. the direct debit prices which we used in Table 6.2), but also lowest and highest prices. Figure 6.9 therefore takes the differential between the highest and lowest prices as an indicator of the degree to which competition is bringing about price convergence in the different customer categories.

---

4   Note that the DTI is still the source for the Eurostat data.

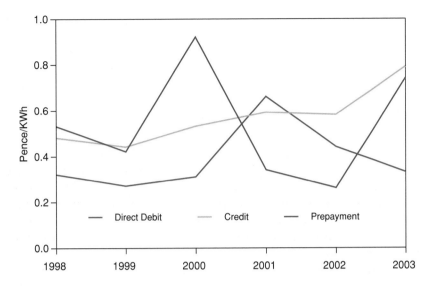

Figure 6.9: Highest minus Lowest Domestic Unit Prices by Customer Category
1998–2003

Source: DTI (2005c)

The particular revelation in this Figure is that the degree of competition does appear to have increased for direct debit customers following the complete removal of price controls in April 2002 (the differential between the highest and lowest prices being paid approximately halved). On the other hand, credit and pre-payment customers had the opposite experience – the degree of competitive pressure on suppliers was sufficiently weak to allow them to increase differentials for these customers.

Conclusions

Out of the complex detail of this and previous chapters, the conclusions from this chapter, at the end of the gas chain, are relatively clear and straightforward. The wholesale market shocks which we analysed in Chapter 4 do percolate through to final prices for larger non-domestic market consumers, but this impact is mitigated by the extent to which competition compels suppliers to at least partially absorb such shocks by reducing or even eliminating their mark-ups. Suppliers have a number of ways of handling the latter risk, including making profits from increasingly excitable futures, forward trading and holding an upstream position. This chapter however highlights the role played by small consumers, particularly captive domestic consumers. Domestic prices have not been immediately responsive to wholesale price shocks because suppliers have established supply mark-ups substantially above what was previously required for a single monopoly supplier of the residential market. As we have seen, OFGAS estimated the supply mark-up to be 10 percent in 1995, while our own calculations indicate that the full liberalisation of the domestic market has been accompanied by an increase to over 20 percent in 2002, 2003 and 2004. While some of this difference will of course be due to the higher cost of supply competition compared with monopoly distribution, it also reflects the cost of managing the risks of liberalisation all along the gas chain.

CHAPTER 7

CONCLUSIONS AND POLICY PERSPECTIVES

Markets and Insecurity of Supply

The relationship between security of supply and markets is usually contemplated in terms of whether or not markets can assure security of supply. Here though the focus has been on the flip-side of this discussion – on the interplay between insecurities of supply and markets. And the evidence suggests that it is insecurities of gas supply, coming in different guises, which have been mainly responsible for the behaviour of UK wholesale prices – in ways mediated by timing, contracts, balancing and the transportation and storage infrastructure. Regulated transportation costs not having exercised any major influence over price during the last five years, it has then been the behaviour of incumbent gas suppliers which has had most influence over prices at the 'burner tip', for businesses and households.

However, while such a brief statement may at one level usefully summarise what has gone before, it ignores an ingredient without which UK gas prices would have behaved fundamentally differently. It is *liberalisation*, involving the fragmentation of the gas chain, the marketisation of relationships which were previously administrative and the atomisation of supply which has provided the critical catalyst. It is liberalisation which has made prices highly sensitive to actual and potential insecurities of supply and which has transformed contracts, the implications of timing and the way in which the transportation and storage infrastructure is used.

This second level of summary does however beg a significant and important question – is liberalisation really the culprit or is the real problem that markets have *not been working properly?* For those who believe that high prices are automatically indicative of market abuse, this tends to be the diagnosis, and a sense that the UK gas market had not been working properly certainly drove the OFGEM probe into wholesale prices. The same perspective also finds its way strongly into the recent UK Parliamentary enquiry into *Fuel Prices* (House of Commons 2005), particularly as articulated by evidence from Energywatch, the consumer protection body. Both of these enquiries, although they came up with limited recommendations which we shall discuss in the next section, more or less grudgingly conceded a clean bill of health in terms of market malfunction related to corporate misbehaviour. For example, according to the Parliamentary enquiry,

> We received no evidence that producers have withheld supply from the market to drive prices up. None of our witnesses has suggested collusion or any other illegal behaviour in the offshore production market; nor do we consider that the sharing of information between companies owning or making use of the same facilities is improper or unnecessary. (House of Commons: p.51, para. 13)

Do we now have any different responses to this question of market malfunction?

One response is purely abstract – that in order to know whether a market has a problem one needs to know what a market working properly would look like, a concept which economists have only ever been able to situate in unreal worlds rather than in a real-life and specific industry like gas. Engaging with the latter, as we have done in this book, we have uncovered no evidence which indicates that the UK market has not been working properly – quite the opposite – it has been working quite properly to the extent that this is possible a) for the natural gas industry in general and b) for the natural gas industry in the UK with its specific sources of supply and its specific configuration of infrastructure. The preceding chapters allow us to demonstrate this from three different perspectives. Firstly, the UK wholesale market has generated clear price signals in response to supply-side problems which are juxtaposed with the relative inflexibility of demand in the short-term. The market has responded to insecurities of supply. The fact that these problems may then, with the benefit of hindsight, appear to have been inflated by forward and futures markets simply reflects a) that this is a commodity with which no uncontracted risks can be taken as far as supplies to consumers are concerned and b) that the risks associated with managing that supply forward are high, such that risk takers do not line up in droves out in the field, but rather prefer to be closer to the barn (particularly since the collapse of Enron in 2001). Moreover, that the risks of managing supply forward are high is not simply a question of the potential physical unreliability of future supplies – it is also down to the fact that liberalised markets impose very high costs on unreliability, both in terms of penalties and thereby in terms of hedging costs. *It has proved costly to replace the administration of risk with the marketisation of risk*, something which was graphically illustrated in Figure 6.2.

Secondly, our evidence suggested that the UK's wholesale gas markets have been working well in another sense. While they experienced initial bouts of turbulence, the volatility of Within-day prices stabilised under both the Flexibility Mechanism and the OCM, and on the OTC. The daily volatility of OTC Day-ahead and Month-ahead prices has been rising but, as one might predict, the volatility of transparent IPE daily trades has been much lower and appears to have stabilised. The Day-ahead prices of both Spectron and Heren appear to move closely together, while the Month-ahead indices of these players and the IPE appear to move perfectly in tandem. The evidence is therefore that in terms of both the transmission and synchronisation (arbitrage) of prices the UK's gas markets have, in a technical sense, been working better as market participants have gained more experience. This is something that would be expected given the relatively small number of market participants and the relative simplicity of marshalling the required information from different markets in one room.

Thirdly, turning to market structure, the outcome which has emerged also reflects the fact that the market has been working well. The positions which companies have taken up in the gas chain reflect the ways that have been open to them for managing risk – for responding to insecurities of supply. Thus companies have, broadly-speaking, either a) hedged with upstream assets b) hedged via a generation portfolio or c) hedged by relying on domestic customers to pay. Some companies display a mixture of one or more of these strategies. Moreover, this process of survival by adapting to the various constraints of a particular market environment is of course not unique to gas and it is also, as we have seen, a feature of the adjacent and inter-linked UK electricity supply industry.

Market Design, Competition and Prices

Exonerating gas markets as they are currently configured is however of little comfort to UK consumers and their representatives, who are becoming increasingly alarmed at the prospect of continuing high gas prices, and particularly about the effects on 'fuel poor' domestic consumers and gas-intensive industries. Indeed, at the time of writing, the Energy Intensive Users' Group has issued a warning that with industrial gas buyers currently having to pay 67 pence per therm for gas to be delivered in the first quarter of 2006, 'compared with about half that price two or three years ago', there is a risk that gas-intensive companies may have to relocate to other countries. Deregulated UK gas prices are even being unfavourably compared with continental

Europe (*Financial Times* 27/7/05). But if there has been no corporate misbehaviour and if the many markets that are articulated with the supply of gas to UK consumers are generating appropriate signals, this leaves only the possibility of alternative market designs – designs which may be broadly categorised into those which involve more competition and those which involve less.

More Competition?

More competition is the reflex of the times. It is expected to make things better and making it happen has become an end in itself, protected by increasingly sophisticated competition law (see, for example, Vickers 2004). But how could the UK gas market actually be made more competitive and, more importantly, would it necessarily bring prices down?

How the UK gas market in general could be made more competitive does in fact encounter objective difficulties. As we saw in Chapter 2, with the exception of supply competition to the domestic market, the ownership structure of the other segments of the gas chain are, or can be represented as, competitive enough to pass muster with the regulatory authorities – otherwise they would surely have been brought to the attention of the Competition Commission. This already suggests that the regulatory authorities (OFGEM, the Office of Fair Trading and the Competition Commission) are toothless to deal with a situation in which ownership structure and behaviour are quite proper, but the overall organisation of company portfolios is such that it can allow gas companies to be profitable whatever the level of gas prices. 'If it is all one company and one chain, how does the market get into that chain?' asked Sir Robert Smith in questioning the OFGEM team during the *Fuel Prices* enquiry (House of Commons 2005: Question 474, 1/2/05).

Secondly, in one of the segments of the gas chain, the industrial and commercial market, it could be argued that competition is quite fierce enough: the atomisation of the supply side brought in by liberalisation transformed the balance of power between buyer and seller, making it very difficult for sellers to make a profit. This is also the message from Figure 6.2, a message which has been underlined by BP's October 2004 decision to exit the smaller end of the industrial and commercial market.

Thirdly, there is the issue of whether there should be intervention to redesign the market if this will have an adverse impact on security of supply. One of our arguments has been that companies have organised themselves in the way that they have in order to be able to supply their customers without interruption and on a long-term basis – that the way in which they are organised to make profits under the constraints which they face is one of the costs of liberalisation which the consumer has to pay, or suffer the consequences of the level of security which lower profits may buy.

These points perhaps explain why the recommendations to come out of the two major enquiries mounted by OFGEM and the UK Parliament leave the UK market virtually undisturbed. Redesign was not among the prescriptions, but more information was, at least for a while. Here the argument was that distrust of the influence of the upstream over prices, and of vertical integration between upstream suppliers and downstream suppliers, could be dispelled by greater transparency, by better information flowing through the market and equally available to all participants. However, the advisability of such an apparently uncontentious idea, which is also theoretically consistent with improving the effectiveness of competition, had already been challenged during the Parliamentary *Fuel Prices* enquiry. Mr Jake Ulrich of Centrica told the enquiry that, 'As an ex-trader responsible for upstream business one thing that is paramount if you do have production problems and you cannot deliver on contract is that you want to be able to go out and buy that replacement gas before the market is aware of it and starts squeezing the price' (House of Commons 2005: response to Question 388, 26/1/05). In other words, if the whole market were to be instantaneously privy to an upstream outage a likely consequence could be even wilder gyrations in prices as everyone piled in to try to profit from the misfortune. Add to this the commercial confidentiality concerns which upstream producers subsequently made clear to OFGEM, and it comes as no surprise that the production flows from offshore platforms will not be wired into the market anytime soon (OFGEM 2005b). Leaving things as they are may mean running the risk that partial information leaks continue to allow selected recipients to manipulate the market, but the alternative of more information, more transparency, more competition could, paradoxically, bring about higher not lower prices.

While prescriptions for the redesign of the UK market may be in short supply, they are not for the continental European market – a major reason why UK consumers have been in trouble, it is suggested, is because the rest of the European Union is not liberalised to the same extent as the UK. OFGEM and the UK government have therefore put a great deal of pressure on the European commission to mount enquiries into competition in the European gas and electricity markets. More competition in continental Europe is seen as coming to the rescue of

UK consumers. Unfortunately this perspective contains sleight of hand and non-sequitur. The sleight of hand is in the way this argument is spuriously linked to the findings of OFGEM's investigation of wholesale prices – when in fact, as we saw in Chapter 4, this investigation found reasonable explanations, unconnected with a lack of liberalisation, to explain why the Interconnector supplies in the autumn of 2003 did not respond promptly to price signals being generated by the UK market. Likewise, if the concern is presented as continental oil-indexed gas contracts which contaminate the UK gas market with oil-linked prices, liberalisation would not necessarily eliminate such contracts and, even if it did, there is no guarantee that this would eliminate the link between oil and gas prices. The non-sequitur is to suggest that greater liberalisation of the European gas market would have the effect of protecting the UK consumer against price escalations. Why would liberalisation not have similar effects in continental Europe to those which it has had in the UK? What if the sort of European supply-side shocks listed by OFGEM as having played a role during the autumn of 2003 (the weather, delayed LNG deliveries, problems with coal barges on the Rhine) were to be immediately reflected in European market sentiment and then transmitted instantly to the UK?

These initiatives, a stifled attempt to introduce greater supply-side transparency and an enquiry by the European Commission (DG Comp) which should report by the end of 2006, exhaust the tabled prescriptions for more competition as an antidote to future price hikes, but they do not exhaust the possibilities. Surely, on several counts, there is a case to be made for greater supply competition in the domestic marketplace? The degree of concentration in this market appears to be dangerously above a desirable level (an HHI of 4049 in December 2003 compared with the 1880 advocated by the Office of Fair Trading), the evidence assembled by OFGEM points to the enduring power of the incumbent (Chapter 3) and our own analysis in Chapter 6 indicates that prices to households could have been raised above the rate of inflation (Figure 6.4) but without good cause in 2002 (Table 6.2, Figure 6.6). Moreover, the evidence in Table 6.2 and Figure 6.6, plus the 2004 increase in British Gas Residential's profits, also indicate that the opportunity to switch supplier has only been creating so much froth on the surface of things: since all price controls on the domestic market were removed, since it was fully liberalised, price increases seem not to have been fully justified by changes in the cost of gas – thereby serving to increase and sustain the supply mark-up. This conclusion, we saw, is corroborated in a different way by OFGEM's own *Domestic Competitive Market Review* which established that there was a substantial amount of 'headroom' in the domestic market for new entrants to come in and discount prices and still make a reasonable profit. There are also issues affecting particular groups of consumers – such as dual fuel deals (OFGEM is concerned) and competition in the markets for credit and pre-payment customers (Figure 6.9).

That reform in the domestic market is not being advocated could be down to the application of competition law in the energy sector. Judgments about abuse of power do not just depend on the mere existence of large market shares in the hands of a few companies: customer behaviour and options and competitor behaviour and capacities are also important (Office of Fair Trading 2001: section 3.22, p.9). However, there is also a major practical issue – retail supply has been shown to be a business that requires the expertise of incumbent gas or electricity companies to handle the number of customers involved and the market has settled down into their hands. What other companies would wish or be able to enter this market, which has also reached maturity? And what advantage for consumers would be served by forcing British Gas to divest more gas customers in addition to the 40 percent which it has already lost? The UK would then lack even one major supplier able to exercise countervailing power with respect to the upstream and to take on major long-term contracts which may be critical to security of supply. In other words, it can be argued that more competition could change the balance of power in the gas chain in a way which would result in higher prices or lower security or both.

Less Competition?

One of our contentions has been that the behaviour of UK gas prices is intimately related to the way in which liberalisation has marketised and made transparent relationships that were previously hidden, administrative and relatively routine. The implications are that these marketised relationships should be replaced by administrative ones, that collaboration should come before competition in this area, that public ownership should supplant private ownership. Moreover, such a prescription may also be reinforced by evidence about the superior price performance of public ownership compared with private ownership – in electricity, for example, from a study comparing French with UK electricity prices since 1990 (Wright and Percebois 2003). While liberalisation can produce dramatic initial reductions in prices for large consumers, particularly the largest, its performance for domestic consumers, such as that revealed in Figure 6.1, may be relatively easily mimicked by a publicly-owned utility.

However, in the UK there is currently no political constituency that would sponsor such a dramatic change in direction, would speak up about the costly and tiring silliness of retail competition for homogeneous products like gas and electricity which are also basic necessities. Instead we must consider the kinds of interventions which may ease the current pain for consumers without demanding any fundamental changes in direction. Two possibilities suggest themselves.

Firstly, price control regulation could be reintroduced for domestic gas (and electricity). While this would of course be more complicated than in its previous incarnation as applied to just a single incumbent, that there is a regulatory appetite for the complexity involved is demonstrated by OFGEM's development of separate regional price controls for the now dismembered gas distribution network (LDZs). Why not also apply the same approach of separate price controls to the relatively small number of major supply companies which now control the domestic market for gas? Such a change would also offer the opportunity to further develop 'comparative regulation' – the relative price regulation (RPR) proposed by Colin Mayer a few years ago as much simpler and more efficient than RPI minus X price regulation (Mayer 2001).

Secondly, to address wholesale market problems, more storage could be contemplated. At the moment there are a number of new storage facilities in the pipeline and the new terminals for LNG imports at Milford Haven and the Isle of Grain will have storage capability, but only two of the dedicated storage facilities are actually under construction (Aldbrough and Humbly Grove) and there is no clear sense of the country developing the storage which it actually needs coming from either OFGEM or the government. The lack of progress on storage since it first warned of a problem in 2002 disappointed the UK Parliament's Trade and Industry Committee as it concluded its recent *Fuel Prices* enquiry (House of Commons 2005: para.10, p.51). However, it is not just the volume of storage which is important – it is the type and its disposition (as we saw in Chapter 1) and who is holding it and for what purpose and with what rules of engagement. And it is the latter (storage ownership, purpose, rules of engagement) which is important for exercising an influence over gas price formation. Ownership of storage space could be by upstream producers, suppliers, the system operator (Transco), the state (strategic storage of gas, just as there is with oil in the USA and other countries), other commercial organisations or a body specially constituted to own and manage gas storage. The purpose and rules of engagement could be market-led or based on coded instructions (e.g. to balance the system). But to try to address the problems of supply-side shocks which have been disturbing the wholesale market and causing forward and futures prices to rocket, a simple idea could be to require upstream producers to hold storage *pro rata* with their production and/or related, for example, to the average volume of production lost due to planned and unplanned maintenance during the last three years. Producers would then be obliged to draw down on this security of supply storage to match any loss of supply caused by offshore field outages. This could go a considerable way towards eliminating minor supply-side shocks which can inflict much damage, and also reassure the markets that significant buffer stocks of gas would be available to assure security of supply during winter months. It would also remove opportunities for profiteering based on privileged access to information about outages.

Market Fundamentals

Of course no amount of market redesign can prevent so-called 'market fundamentals' from exercising their influence over price – and there are two of these which are currently relevant to the price of UK gas in the medium term, and which need to be better understood. One is the relationship between the demand for and the supply of oil: if oil demand continues on its seemingly inexorable upward path, then its effects on prices will continue to spill over into other energy markets, including gas. However, do we know as much as we should about the relationships between oil and gas markets? This book suggests that we don't and that more research is therefore needed, initially to explore the precise linkages which provide transmission mechanisms from one market to the other. Secondly, the prospect is held out before us that the UK need not be concerned about the issues raised in this book because, fairly shortly, the UK gas market will again begin to offer UK consumers the sort of low prices that they have enjoyed since the sixties. This will come about because major new import projects – both pipeline and LNG terminals – will, starting during 2006, bring amounts of gas into the UK which will transform the market. As a pleasing graph in the fifth report from the UK government's Joint Energy Security of Supply Working Group (JESS) shows (DTI 2004b: Box 1, p.14), over the following seven years the UK could have at its disposal at least 50 percent more gas than it would need to meet the highest daily demand that has ever been met to date. The implication is that a glut is approaching which will depress UK gas prices. The problem is that a large part of the glut is approaching in LNG tankers which, as happens regularly with oil tankers, the market may summon elsewhere. Market fundamentals may not therefore behave as we expect them to, forcing us to think again and more radically about the way we have chosen to organise our production and consumption of not just gas, but energy in general. Reinforced by environmental imperatives and supply-side problems which may be both geopolitical and depletion-related, this seems likely to require us to move beyond the current preoccupation with liberalisation in order to focus on bringing about the major investments and changes in behaviour which will serve to first of all control, and then reduce, our demand for energy.

REFERENCES

APX Gas (2004), APX Gas Update September 1st to November 30th 2004, *Transco Operational Forum*, (December 9).

APX Gas (2005a), documents or data accessed at www.apxgas.co.uk or at the former EnMO site www.enmo.co.uk or provided directly to the author by APX Gas.

APX Gas (2005b), APX Gas Update December 1st to 31st 2004, *Transco Operational Forum*, (January 25).

Barcella, M.L. (1999), 'The Pricing of Gas', *Oxford Energy Forum*, Oxford Institute for Energy Studies, (May).

Barton, A.P. and Vermeire, T.A.L. (1999), 'Gas price determination in liberalising markets: lessons from US and UK experience', *British Institute of Energy Economics Annual Conference*, Oxford, St John's College, (September).

BG plc (1997), *Annual Report on Form 20-F.*

BP (2004), *2003 Annual Report on 20-F.*

BP (1997), *Short Term Flat NBP: Contract Terms & Conditions*, London, BP.

British Gas TransCo (1995), *Network Code: the Processes for Gas Transportation Services.*

Centrica (2002), *Annual Report.*

Centrica (2003), *Annual Report.*

Centrica (2004), *Annual Report.*

Competition Commission (2003), Centrica plc and Dynegy Storage Ltd and Dynegy Onshore Processing UK Ltd: A Report on the Merger Situation, London, Competition Commission, (August).

Deloitte (2005), Spectron price data independently published by Deloitte at psg.deloitte.com/spectron/

DTI (Department of Trade & Industry – 2004a), *Joint Energy Security of Supply Working Group: Fourth Report*, (May).

DTI (Department of Trade & Industry – 2004b), *Joint Energy Security of Supply Working Group: Fifth Report*, (November).

DTI (Department of Trade & Industry – 2005a), data from the electronic version of *the UK Digest of Energy Statistics* at www.dti.gov.uk/energy/inform/energy_stats/index.shtml

DTI (Department of Trade & Industry – 2005b), data from the electronic version of *Energy Trends* at www.dti.gov.uk/energy/inform/energy_stats/index.shtml

DTI (Department of Trade & Industry – 2005c), data from the electronic version of *Quarterly Energy Prices* at www.dti.gov.uk/energy/inform/energy_stats/index.shtml

DTI (Department of Trade & Industry – 2005d), data from the Department of Trade & Industry's Oil & Gas division from the menu at www.og.dti.

gov.uk/information

DTI (Department of Trade & Industry – 2005e), data supplied directly to the author by the Department of Trade & Industry.

Dymond, P. (2005), 'Infrastructure Code of Practice', Maclay Murray & Spens Oil & Gas Seminar presentation by the Operations Director of UKOOA, (February 25).

Energy Markets Ltd (2004), Trends in the Price of Gas Futures Contracts in the UK from 1997 to 2003, (January), 13 pp.

EnMO (2003, June 2), 'EnMO steps on the gas and delivers record start to the trading year', Press Release.

Eurostat (2005), data downloaded from http://europa.eu.int/comm/eurostat/suite/retrieve/en/theme8/sirene/es_price/

ExxonMobil (2004), data from www.exxonmobil.com/UK-English/Operation/UK_OP_Off_Gas.asp

Farrington, B. (2004), The Value of Gas Storage in the UK, *Utility Week*, (March 12).

Financial Times (27/7/05), 'Heavy industries fear cold winter could lead to closures', article on p.4 by Rebecca Bream.

FSA (Financial Services Authority 2005), *Analysis of activity in the energy markets 2004*, via www.fsa.gov.uk

Heren Energy (2003), *European Spot Gas Markets*, London, (various issues).

Heren Energy (2005), proprietary data made available to the author by Heren Energy.

House of Commons (2005), *Fuel Prices*, House of Commons Trade & Industry Committee Twelfth Report of Session 2004–05, London, The Stationery Office (HC279).

Huberator (2004), information from www.huberator.com

IEA (1998), *Gas Pricing in Competitive Markets*, OECD/International Energy Agency, Paris.

ILEX (2001), '*What influences gas prices in the UK and why have they increased through 2000?*' paper made available by the Department of Trade & Industry, (January).

IPE (2003), *Pipeline*, International Petroleum Exchange, London.

IPE (2005), proprietary data made available to the author by the International Petroleum Exchange.

Interconnector UK (2004), data from the Interconnector UK website at www.interconnector.co.uk

Iraq Survey Group (2004), Annex F, at http://www.globalsecurity.org/wmd/library/report/2004/isg-final-report/isg-final-report_vol1_rfp-anx-f.htm

Kisero, J. (2004), 'Five-year-old oil contract now faces scrutiny', *Business Week* (Kenya), (February 24) at http://www.nationaudio.com/News/DailyNation/Supplements/bw/current/story240220048.htm

Kuyper, R. (2002), Brent Field Depressurisation, *SHARP IOR eNewsletter*, Issue 2 (May), pp.1–4.

Mayer, C. (2001), 'Water: the 1999 price review', in C. Robinson (ed.), *Regulating*

Utilities: New Issues, New Solutions, Cheltenham, Edward Elgar, Global Energy Policy and Economics Series, pp. 1–20.

Monopolies & Mergers Commission (1993), *Gas and British Gas plc*, Vols 1–3 of reports under the Fair Trading Act 1993 and the Gas Act 1986, London.

Monthly Digest (2004), *Monthly Digest of Statistics*, at www.nationalstatistics.gov.uk, (August).

Mulcare, A. (2001), *The Impact of the UK-Belgium Intercoonnector*, presentation on behalf of Interconnector (UK) Ltd.

National Grid Transco (2003), *Transportation Ten Year Statement*, (December).

National Grid Transco (2004), *Financial News – Sale of four gas distribution networks and proposed £2 billion one-off return of capital to shareholders* at http://production.investis.com/ngt/news/2004/2004-08-31/

National Grid Transco (2005), proprietary data made available to the author by National Grid Transco.

NERA (2002), *Study to Investigate the Likelihood of Firm Load Self-Interruption in a Severe Winter: A Final Report for Transco plc*, London, NERA.

Network Code, Principal Document, version 3.06, issued 28 April 2004 (referred to by alphabetic section), now referred to as the Uniform Network Code which, since May 2005, has been issued by the new Joint Office of Gas Transporters, Solihull.

Office of Fair Trading (2001), *The Competition Act 1998: The application in the Energy Sector*, available via www.oft.gov.uk or ofgem.gov.uk (enforcing competition menu)

OFGAS (various years), *Competitive Market Review*.

OFGAS (1996), *1997 Price Control Review of Supply at or below 2,500 therms a year: The Director General's Initial Proposals*, Vol 1: Consultation Document + Vol 2: Appendices, (June).

OFGAS (1999), *Review of Gas Trading Arrangements: Proposals and Consultation*, (February).

OFGEM (2000a), *The New Gas Trading Arrangements: Further development of the regime: A Decision Document* (February).

OFGEM (2000b), *The New Gas Trading Arrangements: A Review of the New Arrangements and Further Development of the Regime: A Review and Decision Document* (July).

OFGEM (2001a), *The New Gas Trading Arrangements: Further reform of the gas balancing regime: A Consultation Document* (February).

OFGEM (2001b), *Review of Transco's Price Control from 2002: Final Proposals* (September).

OFGEM (2001c), *Review of Transco's Price Control from 2002: Regulatory Instructions and Guidance for Reporting Outputs*, (November).

OFGEM (2001d), *Review of Transco's Price Control from 2002: Initial Thoughts and Consultation Document* (February).

OFGEM (2002a), *The New Gas Trading Arrangements: Reform of the gas balancing regime* Vols 1 & 2, (February).

OFGEM (2002b), Letter from N. Simpson, Director of Industry Code Development, to Shippers, Customers, Transco and other interested parties, Ref NET/COD/GEN1, (November 7).

OFGEM (2002c), *The regulation of Independent Gas Transporter charging*, Consultation document, (May).

OFGEM, (2002d), *Separation of Transco's distribution price control*, Initial consultation document, Office of Gas & Electricity Markets, July.

OFGEM, (2002e), *Separation of Transco's distribution price control*, Draft Proposals, Office of Gas & Electricity Markets, December.

OFGEM (2003a), *The gas trading arrangements: Reform of the gas balancing regime: Next Steps*, (April).

OFGEM (2003b), *Review of Competition in the Non-Domestic Gas and Electricity Supply Sectors*, (July).

OFGEM (2003c), *Publishing information about suppliers' market shares – OFGEM's decision*, (June 11).

OFGEM (2004a), *Wholesale Gas Prices in October and November 2003: Interim Report*, (May).

OFGEM (2004b), *Domestic Competitive Market Review 2004*, (April).

OFGEM (2004c), lists of licensed companies available at www.ofgem.gov.uk

OFGEM (2004d), *OFGEM's probe into wholesale gas prices: Conclusions and Next Steps*, (October).

OFGEM (2004e), *OFGEM's probe into wholesale gas prices: Appendices*, (October).

OFGEM, (2004f), *National Grid Transco–Potential sale of network distribution businesses. agency and governance arrangements*, Regulatory Impact Assessment, Office of Gas & Electricity Markets, (April).

OFGEM, (2004g), *National Grid Transco – Potential sale of gas distribution network business*. Final Impact Assessment, Office of Gas & Electricity Markets, (November).

OFGEM (2004h), *Security of supply October 2003 to March 2004*, Six month retrospective report, (September).

OFGEM (2005a), OFGEM closes Gas Probe, Press Release, 24/6/05.

OFGEM (2005b), Offshore gas production information disclosure: Decision letter, (June).

OPL (Oilfield Publications Ltd – 2003), *The North Sea Field Development Guide*, Ledbury England and Houston, Ninth Edition.

Panagiotidis, T. and E. Rutledge (2004), *Oil and Gas Markets in the UK: Evidence from a Cointegrating Approach*, paper made available by Loughborough University's Department of Economics (October).

Platts (2000), electronic document accessed at http://www.platts.com

Rutledge, I.D. and Wright, P.W. (1997), Comparing The Profitability of British Gas Transco with an International Selection of Gas Transmission Companies, Evidence to the Monopolies & Mergers Commission, (summary published in report on BG plc, pp.256–7).

Rutledge, I.D. and Wright, P.W. (2003), 'Regulation, Competition and Price Formation in the UK Gas Industry', *Economia e politica industriale*, anno XXX no. 120 (December), Milan, IEFE, Bocconi University, pp. 193–208.

RWE (2002), *Annual Report 2002* (English language version).

Thorniley (2004), 'BP abandons small firms to concentrate on bigger picture', *Business.telegraph* at http://www.telegraph.co.uk

Transco (undated), *Summary of the Modification Rules*, (for the Network Code), available from the Transco website at www.transco.co.uk

Transco (2000), *Transco Winter Operations Review 2000*, (undated, probably July).

Transco (2003), *Gas Transportation Charges*, (December).

Transco (2004), *Gas Transportation Charges*, (April).

Transco (various years), *Regulatory Accounting Statements* for financial years 2001/2002, 2002/2003 and 2003/2004.

Transco PGTL, Transco's Public Gas Transporter Licence.

UKOOA (2004), *Code of Practice on Access to Upstream Oil and Gas Infrastructure on the UK Continental Shelf*, London, UK Offshore Operators Assocation.

Vickers, J. (2004), Abuse of market power, Speech to the 31st conference of the European Association for Research in Industrial Economics, Berlin, (September), pp.24.

Wood MacKenzie (2004), data made available to the author by Wood Mac-Kenzie.

Wright, P.W. and Percebois, J. (2003), 'Electricity Consumers under the State and the Private Sector: Comparing the Price Performance of the French and UK Electricity Industries 1990−2000', *Utilities Policy*, Vol 10, No 3, pp. 167−79.

Wright, P.W. (2005), Liberalisation and the Security of Gas Supply in the UK, *Energy Policy*, Vol 33. No 17 (November − advance webcopy available now via Science Direct), pp. 2272−90.

INDEX